WILLIAMS-SONOMA

Fresh & Light

GENERAL EDITOR
Chuck Williams

RECIPES
Lane Crowther

PHOTOGRAPHY
Richard Eskite

TIME LIFE BOOKS

TIME-LIFE BOOKS

Time-Life Books is a division of Time Life Inc.
Time-Life is a trademark of Time Warner Inc. U.S.A

TIME-LIFE CUSTOM PUBLISHING

Vice President and Publisher: Terry Newell
Managing Editor: Donia Ann Steele
Director of Acquisitions: Jennifer L. Pearce
Vice President of Sales and Marketing: Neil Levin
Director of Financial Operations: J. Brian Birky

WILLIAMS-SONOMA

Founder and Vice-Chairman: Chuck Williams
Book Buyer: Victoria Kalish

WELDON OWEN INC.

President: John Owen
Vice President and Publisher: Wendely Harvey
Chief Operating Officer: Larry Partington
Vice President International Sales: Stuart Laurence
Associate Publisher: Lisa Atwood
Managing Editor: Jan Newberry
Consulting Editor: Norman Kolpas
Copy Editor: Sharon Silva
Design: Kari Perin, Perin+Perin
Production Director: Stephanie Sherman
Production Manager: Jen Dalton
Production Editor: Sarah Lemas
Food Stylist: George Dolese
Prop Stylist: Laura Ferguson
Photo Production Coordinator: Juliann Harvey
Photo Assistant: Kevin Hossler
Food Styling Assistant: Jill Sorensen
Glossary Illustrations: Alice Harth

A NOTE ON WEIGHTS AND MEASURES

All recipes include customary U.S. and metric measurements. Metric conversions are based on a standard developed for these books and have been rounded off. Actual weights may vary.

The Williams-Sonoma Lifestyles Series
conceived and produced by Weldon Owen Inc.
814 Montgomery Street, San Francisco, CA 94133

In collaboration with Williams-Sonoma
3250 Van Ness Avenue, San Francisco, CA 94109

Separations by Colourscan Overseas Co. Pte. Ltd.
Printed in Singapore by Tien Wah Press (Pte.) Ltd.

A WELDON OWEN PRODUCTION

Copyright © 1998 Weldon Owen Inc.
All rights reserved, including the right of
reproduction in whole or in part in any form.

First printed in 1998
10 9 8 7 6 5 4 3 2 1

Library of Congress
Cataloging-in-Publication Data

Crowther, Lane.
Fresh & light / general editor, Chuck Williams;
   recipes, Lane Crowther; photography, Richard Eskite.
       p. cm. — (Williams-Sonoma lifestyles)
   Includes index.
   ISBN 0-7835-4617-3
   1. Cookery I. Williams, Chuck. II. Crowther,
Lane. III. Series.
TX714.F746 1998
641.5— dc21   98-9459
                                                 CIP

A NOTE ON NUTRITIONAL ANALYSIS

Each recipe is analyzed for significant nutrients per serving. Not included in the analysis are ingredients that are optional or added to taste, or are suggested as an alternative or substitution either in the recipe or in the recipe introduction or accompanying tip. In recipes that yield a range of servings, the analysis is for the middle of that range. See also page 9.

Contents

Welcome

Not so long ago, if friends told you they were cooking and eating fresh and light food, you would automatically assume they were following some sort of health regimen or diet. But such attitudes have changed.

Today, *fresh* and *light* are two of the adjectives used most often to praise the best contemporary cooking. In fact, almost anyone you ask will admit to trying to eat meals that reflect these two trends. And they do so for different reasons.

Some, of course, have good health in mind, recognizing that countless new studies underscore the benefits of a diet low in animal fats and rich in vegetables and fruits. Others do it to lose weight. I suspect, however, that the majority of people do so for one simple reason: low-fat, high-quality foods, imaginatively prepared, taste great.

This book recognizes that this more sensible approach to cooking can satisfy the needs of many different lifestyles, from helping individuals find information on healthy cooking to giving dieters new low-fat, low-calorie recipes.

I invite you to try these excellent recipes and discover that freshness and lightness are, above all, pleasures to be enjoyed for their own sake.

Chuck Williams

Living Fresh and Light

A bowl of fresh fruit makes a colorful sideboard display (right). Offer the contents of the bowl as a lighter alternative to heavy desserts once the meal is through. Grow thyme, tarragon, and parsley in pots on a kitchen windowsill (below) and fresh, flavorful herbs will always be in reach. Transfer the pots to a tabletop for an easy, informal centerpiece.

Making a Lifestyle Choice

Fresh foods and light cooking go hand in hand. Each on its own provides particular pleasures and benefits; together, they offer not just a way to cook and eat but a way of life.

In this book, *fresh* means in tune with the seasons. Virtually every recipe features peak seasonal produce. Diets rich in fruits and vegetables are naturally healthy, providing plenty of nutrients with less fat and fewer calories.

Light cooking is distinguished by simple preparations that highlight the natural tastes, textures, and colors of fresh vegetables and fruits, as well as good-quality sources of protein such as seafood, poultry, and lean meats. Cooking methods are generally quick, to help keep fresh flavors intact, and require only a minimum of fat (see pages 10–11).

Once you begin to explore the world of fresh ingredients and light cooking, enjoying colorful, flavorful dishes will become a habit, and you will be on the path to a healthier lifestyle.

Seeking Fresh Produce

Any cook interested in preparing fresher, lighter food will first want to find a reliable source for peak-of-the-season produce. Farmers' markets provide an ideal opportunity to buy locally grown fruits

and vegetables directly from the people who grow them. Many food stores and greengrocers also offer a wide variety of fresh, high-quality produce. Of course, for the absolutely freshest produce, there's no better source than a backyard vegetable garden. Even a small patio or balcony can hold a few pots of tomatoes or peppers (capsicums), for example, and any window that gets some sunlight offers a place to grow herbs.

Setting the Fresh and Light Scene

The words *fresh* and *light* sum up the best approach to outfitting the dining table. Simple decorations and table settings complement the food: casual tableware; bowls of fresh fruits and vegetables; bouquets of flowers or herbs.

When it's time to enjoy your fresh and light meal, try one of the beverage recipes featured on pages 14–15, or simply pour a glass of your favorite beer, wine, or mineral water.

NUTRITIONAL ANALYSIS

Each recipe in this book includes a breakdown of calories and common nutrients per serving. Every ingredient is figured into an analysis, except those listed as optional, added to taste, or suggested as substitutions, accompaniments, or garnishes. For advice on what constitutes a healthy diet for you, consult your doctor or other health professional.

Each nutritional analysis provides the following values:

Calories (Kilojoules)
A measure of the energy provided by food. One calorie equals 4.2 kilojoules, an alternative term used in some countries.

Protein
A basic nutrient, protein is essential for building and repairing body tissues and for other important functions.

Carbohydrates
The principal source of dietary energy, classed as either simple (sugars) or complex (starches).

Total Fat and Saturated Fat
Dietary fat, an important source of energy, delivers essential fatty acids and fat-soluble vitamins to the body. Saturated fat, which comes from animals and tropical plants, may be a contributing factor to heart disease.

Cholesterol
Not strictly a fat but a fatlike substance, cholesterol is found only in animal foods, never in plants. While high levels of blood cholesterol can present a risk of cardiovascular disease, dietary cholesterol is not

implicated in raising blood cholesterol. Diets high in saturated fat pose a greater health danger.

Sodium
Essential for regulating the levels of fluids in our bodies. Current research indicates that high-sodium diets are dangerous only for sodium-sensitive individuals.

Dietary Fiber
Made up primarily of complex carbohydrates, dietary fiber is useful for softening and giving bulk to the waste products of digestion.

Keeping It Light

A wealth of readily available ingredients and simple techniques make fresh and light cooking easy. For example, low-fat or nonfat evaporated milk can be whisked into a topping to use instead of high-fat whipped cream (top). With the help of a mandoline or a food processor, summertime squashes (above) can be easily cut into long, thin pastalike strands.

Putting Fat in Perspective

When asked for suggestions on the best way to make food lighter, most people answer "get rid of the fat." Such thinking, however, ignores the legitimate role fat plays in the body's well-being and in making food taste better.

Everyone needs to include some fat in their diet. Our bodies use essential fatty acids to help transport some vitamins through the bloodstream. The fats we eat also help form and maintain the body fat we need for insulation, energy storage, supple skin, and soft, shiny hair. The problem, however, is that many people eat too much fat. Medical experts generally agree that diets high in saturated fat present a risk of cardiovascular disease (see nutritional analysis, page 9).

Fat plays an important role in cooking, too. It makes sauces tastier and thicker and adds richness and body to baked goods and desserts. It also helps transfer heat in cooking, brings out the flavors of herbs and spices, and often contributes a taste of its own.

The key to cooking light, then, is not to eliminate fat completely, but to use it in moderation. Trimming excess fat from meats, reducing the amount of fat called for in recipes, and finding ways to replace fat with other ingredients that add similar richness, body, and flavor are all ways to bring down the level of fats in our diets. Every recipe in this book offers its own small lessons in meeting these challenges.

Trimming Away the Fat

Smart shopping and simple advance preparation can help you reduce the amount of fat in your cooking. First, choose leaner protein sources such as seafood and poultry. When buying meats, look for those without a heavy marbling of fat. Also keep an eye out for meats labeled "lean."

Before cooking, take a few moments to eliminate even more fat. Strip away the skin from poultry and cut away all visible fat from meat.

You'll have another opportunity to get rid of fat after you've cooked a soup, stock, sauce, braise, or stew. Fat rises to the

surface of liquid, where it floats, ready to be skimmed away with a spoon or blotted up with paper towels. If you prepare the dish in advance and refrigerate it, the fat will solidify, making it easy to lift or scrape off.

Making Smart Substitutions

Greater awareness of the health benefits of light cooking has led to the greater availability of products aimed at helping cooks reduce the amount of fat in their cooking.

Nonstick cookware makes it possible to cook with little added fat. And using nonstick cooking spray instead of butter or oil introduces only a trace amount. Occasionally, however, you may want to add a little fat—particularly such flavorful kinds as olive oil, nut oils, or butter—to enhance the overall flavor of a dish or to promote browning.

Reduced-fat or nonfat dairy products can enrich recipes without substantially increasing their fat or cholesterol levels. Most food stores today carry such items as creamy-tasting fat-free evaporated skimmed milk and fat-free sour cream.

Savvy cooks have also learned to replace fat-laden ingredients with other products that yield similar effects. In place of cream, for example, soups or sauces can be enriched with a mixture of low-fat milk and cornstarch, with bread crumbs, or with puréed starchy vegetables or rice. Fruit nectars can replace oil in salad dressings. Puréed fruit or sweet potatoes or fat-free sour cream can lend body to baked goods. Keep in mind, too, the intriguing, fat-free flavors that lively seasonings such as fresh herbs, chiles, or citrus zests can contribute, and you realize how easy it can be to cook lighter food without ever feeling deprived at the table.

A variety of flavorful ingredients can enrich dishes without adding fat. Stock enhances the natural flavors of soups, side dishes, and sauces. Use pear or mango nectar instead of oil in salad dressings. And sometimes, a twist of lemon is often all that is needed to balance the flavors of fresh and light cuisine.

Adding Flavor

By using vivid-tasting ingredients and special cooking techniques, you can introduce bright flavors to your food and reduce the need for additional fat. Try cooking with familiar ingredients that deliver a full-bodied taste, such as the fresh herbs used in Herb-Crusted Beef Medallions (below, right; page 52), fresh and dried chiles, ground and whole spices, citrus juice or zest, or tropical fruits. Or experiment with seasonings from other cuisines, such as those used below to flavor fat-free mayonnaise for Asian Tuna Burgers (page 55) or a few drops of an intensely flavored oil like hazelnut or Asian sesame. You might also want to make your own vegetable stock (opposite) to use as a base for soups and sauces and to flavor a variety of dishes. Learn, too, to rely on classic cooking techniques that heighten taste while adding little, if any, fat, such as those demonstrated at right.

Juicy, sweet, and aromatic, tropical fruits can add an intense flavor to recipes with a minimum of fat and calories. The pineapple and mango shown here combine with cucumber, red bell pepper (capsicum), lime juice, and cilantro (fresh coriander) to make a lively salsa for Seared Scallops (page 70).

FLAVORING MAYONNAISE

Wasabi paste and finely chopped Japanese pickled ginger whisked into fat-free mayonnaise make a tasty spread for chicken or seafood sandwiches, or to use as a dip for raw vegetables.

COATING WITH HERBS

Coarse dried bread crumbs seasoned with chopped fresh herbs—here, parsley, thyme, and sage—and bound with an egg white make an excellent coating for meats, poultry, and seafood.

Light Cooking Methods to Enhance Fresh Foods

Classic cooking techniques, like the ones demonstrated here, require only a minimum of fat, yet they can bring an added dimension of flavor to reduced-fat recipes.

SEARING

Shown here with Seared Scallops with Tropical Salsa (page 70), quick searing creates a nicely browned, richly flavored exterior.

ROASTING

Cooking in the intense, dry heat of an oven concentrates the flavors of seafood, poultry, meat, and, shown here, vegetables.

DEGLAZING AND REDUCING

Using a liquid to dissolve the glaze of juices and dislodge the browned-on bits of food left behind after frying or sautéing recaptures their flavor for an easy sauce. Reducing the liquid by boiling concentrates its flavor.

CARAMELIZING

When cooked to the point that their natural sugars break down and darken, foods—like the long-cooked onions shown here—begin to caramelize and their flavor changes from sharp to mellow and sweet.

SPRING VEGETABLE STOCK

An array of vegetables, including spring-time asparagus, gives this stock a light and slightly sweet finish that makes it tasty enough to serve in cups as a delicate first course. For a richer flavor, use vegetable or chicken broth in place of 2 cups (16 fl oz/500 ml) of the water.

1 lb (500 g) asparagus
1 large leek, chopped
1 large carrot, chopped
1 small yellow onion, chopped
2 celery stalks, chopped
3 large fresh thyme sprigs
2 bay leaves
8 cups (64 fl oz/2 l) water

❀ *Trim the tips from the asparagus and reserve them to blanch and use as a garnish for other recipes. In a large saucepan over high heat, combine the asparagus spears, leek, carrot, onion, celery, thyme, bay leaves, and water. Bring to a boil, reduce the heat to medium, and simmer, uncovered, until reduced to about 5 cups (40 fl oz/1.25 l), about 50 minutes.*

❀ *Remove from the heat. Strain through a sieve and use immediately. Or transfer to a container, cover, and refrigerate for up to 5 days or freeze for up to 2 months.*

MAKES ABOUT 5 CUPS
(40 FL OZ/1.25 L)

Beverages

With an ice bucket, corkscrew, and serving tray on hand, you can serve beverages almost anywhere (top). A whole mint leaf or a thin slice of lemon frozen inside of ice cubes is a refreshing way to dress up cocktails, fresh juices, or iced tea.

Pink Lady Frappé

Strawberries give this cool refreshing drink a lovely blush. Enjoy it as a quick, easy-to-fix breakfast, as a midday snack, or even for dessert.

2½ cups (15 oz/470 g) chopped pineapple
2 cups (8 oz/250 g) strawberries, stems removed
¾ cup (6 fl oz/180 ml) pineapple juice or mango nectar
about 18 ice cubes

❀ In a blender, combine the pineapple, strawberries, and juice or nectar. Purée until smooth and thick. Add the ice cubes and purée until slushy.

❀ Divide among glasses and serve immediately.

SERVES 6

Blackberry Limeade

Boysenberries, blueberries, or other dark berries can be substituted for the blackberries. Frozen berries, which are often sweeter than fresh ones, will also yield excellent results.

2 cups (8 oz/250 g) blackberries, plus 8 berries
1 cup (8 fl oz/250 ml) lime juice, plus 1 lime, cut into 8 thin slices
½ cup (6 oz/185 g) honey
2 cups (16 fl oz/500 ml) water
ice cubes

❀ In a blender, combine the 2 cups (8 oz/250 g) berries, lime juice, and honey. Process to a smooth purée. Strain through a fine-mesh sieve into a pitcher or jar, pressing firmly against the solids with the back of a spoon to extract as much juice as possible. Stir in the water, cover, and refrigerate until well chilled, about 2 hours.

❀ Fill tall glasses with ice cubes. Then divide the limeade evenly among the glasses. Spear 2 berries and 2 lime slices onto each of 4 small wooden skewers and use to garnish the glasses. Serve immediately.

SERVES 4

Vanilla Bean and Mint Iced Tea

This refreshing iced tea offers a cooling counterpoint to spicy dishes like the Bangkok Chicken Salad (page 34).

5 cups (40 fl oz/1.25 l) water
⅓ cup (½ oz/15 g) firmly packed fresh
   mint leaves, plus 4 small sprigs
⅓ cup (3 oz/90 g) sugar
½ vanilla bean, split lengthwise
4 orange-spice tea bags
ice cubes

❊ In a saucepan over medium-high heat, combine the water, mint leaves, and sugar. Using the tip of a sharp knife, scrape the vanilla seeds from the bean halves into the pan, then toss in the bean as well. Bring to a boil, stirring to dissolve the sugar. Remove from the heat, add the tea bags, cover, and let steep for 10 minutes. Strain through a fine-mesh sieve into a pitcher or jar, pressing firmly against the solids with the back of a spoon to extract as much flavor as possible. Return the vanilla bean to the tea. Cover and refrigerate until well chilled, at least 4 hours or as long as overnight.

❊ Fill tall glasses with ice cubes, then divide the tea evenly among the glasses, discarding the bean. Garnish with the mint sprigs and serve immediately.

SERVES 4

Chocolate-Banana Smoothie

This maltlike concoction delivers a quick energy-boost—perfect before or after a visit to the gym.

2 very ripe bananas
¾ cup (6 fl oz/180 ml) low-fat milk
⅔ cup (5 fl oz/160 ml) frozen fat-free
   chocolate yogurt

❊ Peel the bananas, wrap tightly in plastic wrap, and freeze until solid, 4–5 hours.

❊ Break the bananas into large chunks and place in a blender. Add the milk and yogurt, and purée until smooth and thick.

❊ Divide between tall glasses and serve immediately.

SERVES 2

Planning Menus

The recipes in this book can be mixed and matched to create a wide range of menus for any occasion. The ten menus here offer only a handful of the many possible combinations you can compose from these pages. When planning any menu, choose courses whose ingredients, seasonings, textures, and colors complement one another. Add other components, as you wish, such as green salads, vegetable accompaniments, fresh-baked breads, and beverages.

Elegant Dinner Party

Smoked Salmon with
Mustard-Dill Potatoes
PAGE 33

Caramelized Veal Chops
with Balsamic Syrup
PAGE 42

Mocha Cake with
Caramel-Spiced Sauce
PAGE 96

Fresh Southwestern Lunch

Butternut Squash and
Chipotle Soup
PAGE 23

Southwest Caesar Salad
PAGE 30

Fresh Seasonal Fruits

Casual Autumn Supper

Warm Mushroom Salad with
Shallot Vinaigrette
PAGE 38

Chicken Paupiettes with
Lemon-Tarragon Sauce
PAGE 48

Caramelized
Spiced Apple Tartlets
PAGE 107

Roasted Asparagus and Shrimp Chowder

PREP TIME: 20 MINUTES

COOKING TIME: 35 MINUTES

INGREDIENTS

10 large asparagus spears, tough ends removed (see tip)

20 large shrimp (prawns), about 1 lb (500 g) total weight, peeled and deveined

2 teaspoons olive oil

1 small fennel bulb

1 leek, including 2 inches (5 cm) of green, chopped

1 small red bell pepper (capsicum), seeded and chopped

1 teaspoon herbes de Provence

3 cups (24 fl oz/750 ml) Spring Vegetable Stock (page 13) or broth

1 russet potato, unpeeled, cut into ½-inch (12-mm) dice

1 cup (8 fl oz/250 ml) fat-free evaporated skimmed milk

salt and ground pepper to taste

PREP TIP: To trim asparagus, simply grasp the spear with both hands and snap it; it will break at the point at which the stalk turns tender. Do not discard too much of the stalk as it's usually a little bit sweeter than the tips.

Roasting the asparagus and shrimp gives an intense flavor to this colorful chunky soup. Reserve the feathery tops from the fennel bulb and use them as a garnish.

SERVES 6

❋ Preheat an oven to 425°F (220°C).

❋ Place the asparagus and the shrimp on a baking sheet and drizzle with the olive oil. Toss to coat them with the oil and then spread out in a single layer.

❋ Roast until the shrimp turn pink and opaque, about 5 minutes. Transfer to a plate. Turn the asparagus over and continue to roast until just tender, about 8 minutes longer. Remove from the oven and, when cool enough to handle, cut into 1-inch (2.5-cm) lengths.

❋ Meanwhile, cut off the stems, feathery tops, and any bruised outer stalks from the fennel bulb. Reserve the tops. Cut away and discard the core, then chop the bulb; set aside.

❋ Heat a large saucepan over medium heat. Coat the pan with nonstick cooking spray. Add the fennel, leek, red pepper, and herbes de Provence and sauté until the vegetables are just beginning to soften, about 4 minutes. Add the stock or broth and potato and bring to a simmer. Cook, uncovered, until the fennel is tender, about 15 minutes.

❋ Pour in the milk and bring the soup back to a simmer. Add the shrimp and asparagus and stir until heated through. Season with salt and pepper.

❋ Ladle into warmed bowls. Garnish each serving with the reserved fennel tops. Serve hot.

NUTRITIONAL ANALYSIS PER SERVING: Calories 174 (Kilojoules 731); Protein 19 g; Carbohydrates 19 g; Total Fat 3 g; Saturated Fat 0 g; Cholesterol 95 mg; Sodium 183 mg; Dietary Fiber 2 g

Chilled Cucumber Soup with Radish Confetti

PREP TIME: 15 MINUTES,
    PLUS 30 MINUTES FOR
    CHILLING

INGREDIENTS

2 lb (1 kg) cucumbers, peeled, halved, and seeded

⅓ cup (1½ oz/45 g) chopped yellow onion

1 cup (8 fl oz/250 ml) low-fat buttermilk

½ cup (4 oz/125 g) fat-free plain yogurt

salt and ground pepper to taste

⅓ cup (1½ oz/45 g) diced radish

¼ cup (¾ oz/20 g) finely chopped green (spring) onion tops

This light and refreshing soup is a delicious start to a meal. Serve it with grilled salmon and Artichoke and Radicchio Barley "Risotto" (page 83). For other colorful garnishes, try shredded carrots, or finely diced tomato. Chopped fresh dill may be substituted for the green (spring) onions.

SERVES 4

❋ Finely dice enough cucumber to measure ⅓ cup (2 oz/60 g); set aside. Chop the remaining cucumber and place in a blender or food processor with the onion, buttermilk, and yogurt. Process until smooth. Season with salt and pepper. Cover and refrigerate until cold, about 30 minutes.

❋ To serve, divide the soup among chilled bowls and garnish with the reserved cucumber, the radish, and the green onion. Serve at once.

NUTRITIONAL ANALYSIS PER SERVING: Calories 80 (Kilojoules 336); Protein 5 g; Carbohydrates 13 g; Total Fat 1 g; Saturated Fat 0 g; Cholesterol 4 mg; Sodium 124 mg; Dietary Fiber 2 g

Butternut Squash and Chipotle Soup

PREP TIME: 15 MINUTES

COOKING TIME: 1¼ HOURS

INGREDIENTS

1 butternut squash, 2½ lb (1.25 kg)

1 tablespoon corn oil

2 slices coarse country bread, each about ½ inch (12 mm) thick, cut into ½-inch (12-mm) cubes

1 teaspoon dried sage

½ yellow onion, chopped

2 small chipotle chiles (see tip)

3½ cups (28 fl oz/875 ml) chicken broth

salt to taste

fresh sage leaves (optional)

PREP TIP: In this soup, you can use either canned chipotles or the ones sold loose.

A sweet, mild purée of butternut squash provides the perfect backdrop for the intriguing smoky, spicy flavor of chipotle chiles. Serve this satisfying soup with Southwest Caesar Salad (page 30) for a casual lunch or light supper.

SERVES 6

❀ Preheat an oven to 350°F (180°C). Cut the squash in half lengthwise. Using a spoon, scrape out the seeds and any fibers and discard. Place the squash halves, cut sides down, on a baking sheet and bake until just tender, about 35 minutes. Remove from the oven. When cool enough to handle, scoop out the flesh into a bowl.

❀ In a large saucepan over medium-high heat, warm the corn oil. Add the bread and dried sage and sauté, stirring often, until the bread cubes are browned on all sides, about 4 minutes. Using a slotted spoon, transfer the croutons to a plate and set aside. Add the onion to the pan and sauté until softened, about 5 minutes. Stir in the squash, chiles, and broth. Bring to a simmer over medium heat and cook, uncovered, until the squash is very soft, about 30 minutes.

❀ If using dried chiles, remove them from the pan, cut away their stems, then return the chiles to the soup. Working in batches, purée the soup in a blender until smooth. Taste and add salt as needed.

❀ If the soup has cooled, return it to the pan and reheat gently. Ladle into warmed bowls. Divide the croutons among the servings and garnish with the sage leaves, if desired. Serve hot.

NUTRITIONAL ANALYSIS PER SERVING: Calories 139 (Kilojoules 584); Protein 4 g; Carbohydrates 25 g; Total Fat 4 g; Saturated Fat 1 g; Cholesterol 2 mg; Sodium 117 mg; Dietary Fiber 3 g

Caramelized Red Onion Soup with Goat Cheese Crostini

PREP TIME: 20 MINUTES

COOKING TIME: 50 MINUTES

INGREDIENTS

3 red (Spanish) onions, thinly sliced

4 cloves garlic, thinly sliced

2 teaspoons brown sugar

I teaspoon dried thyme

salt and ground pepper to taste

I cup (8 fl oz/250 ml) dry red wine

3 cups (24 fl oz/750 ml) chicken
  broth

¼ cup (2 oz/60 g) herb-flavored soft
  goat cheese

8 slices baguette, each about ½ inch
  (12 mm) thick, toasted

fresh thyme sprigs (optional)

Long cooking intensifies the natural sweetness of the onions and deepens the flavor of this soup—a contemporary interpretation of the French bistro classic. Just a little bit of goat cheese goes a long way toward enriching this light soup.

SERVES 4

❀ Heat a heavy saucepan over medium heat. Coat the pan with nonstick cooking spray. Add the onions, garlic, sugar, and thyme, and season with salt and pepper. Cook, stirring often, until the onions are quite soft but haven't begun to color, about 25 minutes.

❀ Pour in the wine and deglaze the pan, stirring with a wooden spoon to remove any browned bits from the pan bottom. Simmer over medium heat until the liquid has evaporated, about 15 minutes.

❀ Add the broth and simmer over medium heat until reduced to about 4 cups (32 fl oz/1 l), about 10 minutes. Meanwhile, spread the goat cheese on the toasted bread slices.

❀ Ladle the soup into warmed bowls. Float 2 toasts in each bowl. Garnish the toasts with thyme sprigs, if desired. Serve hot.

NUTRITIONAL ANALYSIS PER SERVING: Calories 284 (Kilojoules 1193); Protein 12 g; Carbohydrates 47 g; Total Fat 6 g; Saturated Fat 3 g; Cholesterol 18 mg; Sodium 481 mg; Dietary Fiber 4 g

Purée of Snow Pea and Leek Soup

PREP TIME: 30 MINUTES

COOKING TIME: 20 MINUTES

INGREDIENTS

2 leeks, including 2 inches (5 cm) of green, chopped

2 teaspoons sugar

¾ lb (375 g) snow peas (mangetouts), trimmed

3 cups (24 fl oz/750 ml) chicken broth

½ cup (4 fl oz/125 ml) low-fat milk

salt and ground white pepper

¼ cup (2 oz/60 g) fromage blanc

1 teaspoon chopped fresh tarragon

SERVING TIP: For a more elegant presentation, try spooning the tarragon-cheese garnish onto the soup in small dots. Then pull the tip of a small knife through the dots to make a pattern of swirls across the surface.

For the best flavor, be sure to select young, tender snow peas. This soup can also be refrigerated and served chilled; if you do, taste and adjust the seasoning before serving.

SERVES 4

❋ Place a heavy saucepan over medium heat. Coat the pan with non-stick cooking spray. Add the leeks, sprinkle with the sugar, and sauté, stirring frequently, until softened, about 8 minutes. Do not allow the leeks to color. Add the snow peas and sauté until they turn bright green, about 4 minutes. Remove 8 snow peas and set aside.

❋ Add the broth to the pan and bring to a simmer. Simmer, uncovered, over medium heat until the peas are quite tender, about 8 minutes longer. Remove from the heat.

❋ Purée the soup in a blender until smooth. Pour through a sieve placed over a clean saucepan, pressing hard on the solids with the back of a spoon. Discard the solids. Stir the milk into the purée and reheat gently. Season generously with salt and white pepper.

❋ Meanwhile, in a small bowl, stir together the fromage blanc and tarragon. Season with white pepper. Cut the reserved snow peas into thin strips.

❋ Ladle the soup into warmed bowls. Place a dollop of the fromage blanc on top of each serving and garnish with the julienned snow peas. Serve hot.

NUTRITIONAL ANALYSIS PER SERVING: Calories 123 (Kilojoules 517); Protein 8 g; Carbohydrates 20 g; Total Fat 2 g; Saturated Fat 1 g; Cholesterol 5 mg; Sodium 146 mg; Dietary Fiber 3 g

Mesclun, Arugula, and Fennel Salad with Prosciutto and Pear Vinaigrette

PREP TIME: 15 MINUTES

INGREDIENTS

⅔ cup (5 fl oz/160 ml) pear nectar

¼ cup (2 fl oz/60 ml) seasoned rice vinegar

salt and ground pepper to taste

1 fennel bulb

5 oz (155 g) mesclun salad greens

1 cup (1 oz/30 g) arugula (rocket) leaves, torn into pieces

2 oz (60 g) thinly sliced prosciutto, julienned

4 figs, quartered through the stem end

1 oz (30 g) Parmesan cheese

PREP TIP: The inner layers of a fennel bulb are the tenderest part. Depending on the size and maturity of your particular bulb, you may want to discard the thick outer layer and use only the tender center. If the fennel is stringy, you can strip the strings off with a vegetable peeler.

A trio of taste sensations—sweet, sour, salty—and a host of exotic flavors come together in this salad. It is simple to make, but it demands the very best ingredients you can find. Mesclun, a mix of young, tender salad greens, is available from high-quality greengrocers. Seek out prosciutto and Parmesan cheese imported from Italy.

SERVES 4

⊛ In a small bowl, stir together the pear nectar and vinegar. Season with salt and pepper. Set the dressing aside.

⊛ Cut off the stems and feathery tops and any bruised outer stalks from the fennel bulb. Reserve the tops. Cut the fennel bulb in half lengthwise and cut away and discard the core. Slice crosswise paper-thin. Set aside.

⊛ In a bowl, combine the mesclun and arugula. Add half of the dressing and toss well. Place the greens on individual plates, dividing them evenly. Top the greens with the fennel, prosciutto, and figs, and drizzle with the remaining dressing. Using a cheese plane or a vegetable peeler, shave thin slices from the cheese and sprinkle over the salads. Season with pepper and serve.

NUTRITIONAL ANALYSIS PER SERVING: Calories 150 (Kilojoules 630); Protein 8 g; Carbohydrates 22 g; Total Fat 4 g; Saturated Fat 2 g; Cholesterol 16 mg; Sodium 726 mg; Dietary Fiber 3 g

Southwest Caesar Salad

INGREDIENTS

¼ cup (2 fl oz/60 ml) lime juice

4 teaspoons olive oil

3 large cloves garlic, minced

1 tablespoon chili powder

2 teaspoons ground cumin

1½ teaspoons Worcestershire sauce

2 heads romaine (cos) lettuce,
  leaves separated, or 1 large head,
  leaves separated and torn into
  pieces

1 cup (4 oz/125 g) crumbled cotija
  cheese (see note)

1 jicama, ¾ lb (375 g), peeled and
  cut into ½-inch (12-mm) cubes

ground pepper to taste

PREP TIP: Before you bring a jicama
home, scratch the skin with your
fingernail; the skin should be thin
and the flesh beneath it should be
creamy and juicy. A vegetable peeler
does a poor job of peeling jicama;
use a paring knife instead to remove
all the brown skin and the fibrous
layer beneath it.

Jicama, a sweet and crunchy tuber, plays the role of the croutons in this Tex-Mex variation of the classic salad. If you are a fan of anchovies, add a few coarsely chopped ones along with the lettuce; or garnish individual salads with a few whole anchovy fillets. Instead of the traditional croutons, you could garnish the salad with oven-baked potato chips. Mexican *cotija*, a dry part-skim-milk cheese, replaces the usual Parmesan cheese. If you can't find it at your market, use a low-fat feta cheese instead.

SERVES 6

❋ In a large bowl, combine the lime juice, olive oil, garlic, chili powder, cumin, and Worcestershire sauce. Stir to mix well.

❋ Add the lettuce, cheese, and jicama and toss to combine and coat all the leaves. Season generously with pepper and serve.

NUTRITIONAL ANALYSIS PER SERVING: Calories 142 (Kilojoules 596); Protein 7 g; Carbohydrates 10 g; Total Fat 9 g; Saturated Fat 4 g; Cholesterol 15 mg; Sodium 370 mg; Dietary Fiber 5 g

Smoked Salmon with Mustard-Dill Potatoes

PREP TIME: 20 MINUTES

COOKING TIME: 20 MINUTES

INGREDIENTS

1¼ lb (625 g) baby red new potatoes

⅓ cup (3 oz/90 g) fromage blanc

2½ tablespoons chopped fresh dill, plus sprigs for garnish (optional)

1 teaspoon mustard seeds

ground pepper to taste

¼ cup (2 oz/60 g) Dijon mustard

¼ cup (2 fl oz/60 ml) fat-free sour cream

1½ tablespoons sugar

4 teaspoons white wine vinegar

½ lb (250 g) thinly sliced smoked salmon

fresh dill sprigs (optional)

Nearly any type of smoked salmon will work well here. For a special occasion, use good-quality Scottish smoked salmon. Serve with pumpernickel toast points, if desired.

SERVES 4

❊ Place the potatoes in a saucepan with boiling water to cover. Reduce the heat to medium and simmer, uncovered, until just tender, about 20 minutes. Drain and transfer to a work surface.

❊ Meanwhile, in a small bowl, combine the fromage blanc, ½ tablespoon of the chopped dill, and the mustard seeds and stir until smooth. Season with pepper and set aside.

❊ In a bowl, stir together the mustard, sour cream, the remaining 2 tablespoons dill, sugar, and vinegar. Cut the potatoes into slices ¼ inch (6 mm) thick, add to the mustard mixture, and toss gently to coat. Season with pepper.

❊ Transfer the potatoes to individual plates, dividing them evenly. Top with the salmon; drizzle the fromage blanc mixture on top of the salmon. Garnish with dill sprigs, if desired.

NUTRITIONAL ANALYSIS PER SERVING: Calories 252 (Kilojoules 1058); Protein 16 g; Carbohydrates 35 g; Total Fat 3 g; Saturated Fat 1 g; Cholesterol 16 mg; Sodium 943 mg; Dietary Fiber 2 g

Bangkok Chicken Salad

PREP TIME: 45 MINUTES,
PLUS 20 MINUTES FOR
MARINATING

COOKING TIME: 20 MINUTES

INGREDIENTS

1 lb (500 g) skinless, boneless chicken breast halves

⅓ cup (½ oz/15 g) chopped fresh mint

¼ cup (1¼ oz/37 g) peeled and minced fresh ginger

3 large cloves garlic, minced

1 large jalapeño chile, minced

¼ cup (2 fl oz/60 ml) reduced-sodium soy sauce

3 tablespoons lime juice

3 tablespoons honey

2 teaspoons Asian sesame oil

1 head napa cabbage, 1¼ lb (625 g)

3 oz (90 g) dried rice noodles

2 cucumbers, peeled, halved, seeded, and sliced

2 cups (10 oz/310 g) shredded carrots

6 green (spring) onions, chopped

PREP TIP: A small metal spoon is a handy tool for peeling ginger. Just use the tip of it to scrape the peel away. You'll lose only the peel and none of the flavorful ginger itself.

This refreshing and spicy salad is even easier to make with leftover cooked chicken breasts and store-bought shredded carrots. Dried rice noodles are sometimes called *maifun* or rice vermicelli. You can also use bean thread noodles, sometimes called *saifun* or cellophane noodles; these become translucent when cooked.

SERVES 8 AS A FIRST COURSE OR 4 AS A MAIN COURSE

❀ Preheat an oven to 375°F (190°C). Place the chicken in a single layer on a baking sheet. Cover with aluminum foil. Bake until cooked through, about 15 minutes. Remove from the oven, discard the foil, and let cool. Shred the meat; set aside.

❀ In a bowl, stir together the mint, ginger, garlic, chile, soy sauce, lime juice, honey, and sesame oil. Set aside.

❀ Remove 8 of the outer leaves from the cabbage head and reserve. Cut out the core and then finely shred the remaining leaves; you should have about 4 cups (12 oz/375 g). Set aside.

❀ Bring a large saucepan three-fourths full of water to a boil. Add the noodles and cook until tender, about 4 minutes. Drain and rinse under cold running water. Drain again and cut into 2-inch (5-cm) lengths.

❀ In a large bowl, combine the shredded cabbage, chicken, cucumbers, carrots, green onions, noodles, and soy sauce mixture. Let stand for 20 minutes to allow the flavors to blend.

❀ Line a serving bowl with the reserved cabbage leaves. Mound the salad in the center. Serve immediately.

NUTRITIONAL ANALYSIS PER SERVING: Calories 170 (Kilojoules 714); Protein 15 g; Carbohydrates 24 g; Total Fat 2 g; Saturated Fat 0 g; Cholesterol 33 mg; Sodium 372 mg; Dietary Fiber 2 g

Curried Crab Salad with Mango-Mojo Sauce

PREP TIME: 30 MINUTES

INGREDIENTS

1 lb (500 g) asparagus, tough ends removed

1 mango, peeled, pitted, and sliced

1 tablespoon lime juice

1 small clove garlic, chopped

¾ teaspoon ground cumin

¼ cup (2 fl oz/60 ml) water, if needed

½ lb (250 g) fresh-cooked crabmeat, broken into pieces

1 cup (5 oz/155 g) peeled, seeded, and chopped cucumber

⅓ cup (3 fl oz/80 ml) fat-free mayonnaise

¼ cup (⅓ oz/10 g) snipped fresh chives, plus extra for garnish, if desired

1½ teaspoons curry powder

salt and ground pepper to taste

Lime juice, garlic, oregano, and cumin are some of the seasonings often found in the archetypal Cuban spiced vinaigrette known as *mojo*. Those same flavors, combined with a purée of sweet and aromatic fresh mango, give this sophisticated seafood salad a refreshing kick.

SERVES 4

❀ Bring a saucepan three-fourths full of water to a boil. Add the asparagus and boil for 3 minutes. Drain and immerse in cold water to stop the cooking. Drain again. Cut all but 8 of the asparagus on the diagonal into ¾-inch (2-cm) lengths. Set aside.

❀ In a blender, combine the mango, lime juice, garlic, and cumin. Blend until smooth. If the mixture is too thick, thin to a sauce consistency with the water. Set aside.

❀ In a bowl, combine the cut asparagus, crabmeat, cucumber, mayonnaise, ¼ cup (⅓ oz/10 g) chives, and curry powder. Mix well and season to taste with salt and pepper.

❀ Arrange the crab salad on a plate. Garnish with the reserved asparagus slices and a sprinkling of chives and serve. Pass the sauce at the table.

NUTRITIONAL ANALYSIS PER SERVING: Calories 136 (Kilojoules 571); Protein 15 g; Carbohydrates 17 g; Total Fat 2 g; Saturated Fat 0 g; Cholesterol 57 mg; Sodium 304 mg; Dietary Fiber 2 g

Warm Mushroom Salad with Shallot Vinaigrette

PREP TIME: 20 MINUTES

COOKING TIME: 15 MINUTES

INGREDIENTS

3 large shallots, chopped

3 tablespoons sherry vinegar

¾ cup (6 fl oz/180 ml) chicken broth

salt and ground pepper to taste

5 oz (155 g) assorted baby salad greens

¾ cup (¾ oz/20 g) assorted fresh herb leaves such as tarragon, chive, basil, and parsley, in any combination

2 teaspoons hazelnut oil

1 lb (500 g) assorted fresh mushrooms such as cremini, porcini, morel, chanterelle, shiitake, and oyster, in any combination, brushed clean and quartered

1 package (3½ oz/105 g) enoki mushrooms, trimmed

Serve this salad of mixed mushrooms and fragrant herbs as a robust and earthy beginning to a cool-weather meal. Any assortment of fresh mushrooms will work well.

SERVES 4

✳ In a small saucepan over high heat, combine ¼ cup (1 oz/30 g) of the shallots, the vinegar, and the broth. Bring to a boil and boil until reduced to ¾ cup (6 fl oz/180 ml), about 3 minutes. Season with salt and pepper and set aside.

✳ In a bowl, toss together the salad greens, herb leaves, and hazelnut oil until all the leaves are evenly coated with the oil. Season with salt and pepper; set aside.

✳ Heat a nonstick sauté pan over medium heat. Coat the pan with nonstick cooking spray. Add the remaining shallots and sauté until softened, about 1 minute. Add the heartier mushrooms such as cremini and porcini, and sauté until browned, about 5 minutes. Add the more delicate mushrooms such as morels, chanterelles, and shiitakes, and coat them with nonstick cooking spray. Season with salt and pepper. Sauté until all the mushrooms are just tender, about 3 minutes longer. If using oyster mushrooms, add them during the last minute or two of cooking. Pour in the shallot-vinegar mixture and deglaze the pan, stirring with a wooden spoon to remove any browned bits from the pan bottom.

✳ Divide the greens among individual plates. Top with the warm mushrooms and their juices, dividing evenly. Garnish with the enoki mushrooms. Serve immediately.

NUTRITIONAL ANALYSIS PER SERVING: Calories 77 (Kilojoules 323); Protein 5 g; Carbohydrates 11 g; Total Fat 3 g; Saturated Fat 0 g; Cholesterol 1 mg; Sodium 28 mg; Dietary Fiber 3 g

Ancho Chile Fajitas

PREP TIME: 15 MINUTES,
PLUS 6 HOURS FOR
MARINATING

COOKING TIME: 25 MINUTES

INGREDIENTS

2 cups (16 fl oz/500 ml) water

3 ancho chiles

8 cloves garlic

1 lb (500 g) beef flank steak, trimmed
of fat

4 large Anaheim chiles, sliced
crosswise

2 red bell peppers (capsicums),
seeded and sliced

1 red (Spanish) onion, sliced

1 tablespoon ground cumin

salt and ground pepper to taste

8 fat-free flour tortillas, each 6 inches
(15 cm) in diameter, heated

Suggested condiments: fat-free sour
cream, salsa, chopped green
(spring) onions, chopped fresh
cilantro (fresh coriander), and
lime wedges

Fajitas make a quick-and-easy midweek dinner. Combine the beef and marinade the night before, then you need only assemble the condiments and sauté the meat just before serving. Let your guests garnish and wrap their own fajitas.

SERVES 4

❀ In a saucepan, bring the water to a boil. Remove from the heat and add the ancho chiles. Cover and let stand off the heat until the chiles are soft, about 15 minutes.

❀ Using tongs, remove the chiles from the water; reserve the water. When cool enough to handle, slit the chiles lengthwise and seed them. Discard the stems and seeds. Place the ancho chiles, garlic, and 3 tablespoons of the cooking water in a blender and process until smooth. Set aside.

❀ Place the flank steak in a shallow nonaluminum bowl. Add ⅓ cup (3 fl oz/80 ml) of the ancho purée and turn the steak to coat both sides. Cover the bowl and refrigerate for at least 6 hours or up to overnight. Reserve the remaining purée in a separate covered bowl in the refrigerator.

❀ Heat a large nonstick frying pan over medium heat. Coat with nonstick cooking spray. Add the Anaheim chiles, bell peppers, red onion, cumin, salt, and pepper and sauté until the vegetables are tender, about 25 minutes. Remove from the heat and keep warm.

❀ Meanwhile, heat another nonstick frying pan over medium heat. Coat the pan with nonstick cooking spray. Season the steak with salt, and add to the pan. Cook until the meat is well browned on the first side, about 5 minutes. Turn and continue to cook until well browned on the second side and medium-rare at the center, about 4 minutes longer. Transfer the steak to a cutting board and let rest for several minutes.

❀ Thinly slice the steak across the grain and place in a bowl. Add another 3 tablespoons of the ancho purée and mix well. Transfer the vegetables and the steak to a warmed platter, arranging them separately. Serve with the hot tortillas and the condiments in small bowls for guests to help themselves.

NUTRITIONAL ANALYSIS PER SERVING: Calories 327 (Kilojoules 1373); Protein 28 g; Carbohydrates 31 g; Total Fat 11 g; Saturated Fat 4 g; Cholesterol 57 mg; Sodium 273 mg; Dietary Fiber 6 g

Caramelized Veal Chops with Balsamic Syrup

PREP TIME: 10 MINUTES

COOKING TIME: 15 MINUTES

INGREDIENTS

⅓ cup (3 fl oz/80 ml) balsamic vinegar

2 tablespoons soy sauce

½ cup (4 fl oz/125 ml) orange juice

1 tablespoon sugar

2 teaspoons crushed white peppercorns

4 veal rib chops, 6 oz (185 g) each, trimmed of fat

SERVING TIP: To make orange twists for garnish, use a scorer or channel knife to remove the peel from an orange in a narrow, continuous piece. Wrap the peel tightly around a chopstick, then wrap the chopstick in plastic wrap. Refrigerate for about 1 hour. Unwrap, slip the peel free of the chopstick, and cut into 4 equal pieces. Garnish each chop with a twist.

An easy preparation with an impressive delivery, these veal chops can be regally accompanied with green beans tossed in sesame oil and sesame seeds and mashed sweet potatoes.

SERVES 4

❋ In a small saucepan over medium-high heat, combine the vinegar and soy sauce. Bring to a boil and boil until the liquid is reduced to 3 tablespoons, about 5 minutes. Remove from the heat, stir in the orange juice, and set aside.

❋ In a small bowl, stir together the sugar and peppercorns. Press the sugar mixture onto one side of each veal chop, dividing it evenly.

❋ Heat a large nonstick frying pan over medium-high heat. Coat the pan with nonstick cooking spray. Add the chops, sugar sides down, and cook until caramelized on the first side, about 2 minutes. Turn and continue to cook until pale pink when cut into at the thickest point, about 3 minutes longer.

❋ Transfer the chops to a warmed platter. Return the pan to medium-high heat. Pour in the reduced vinegar mixture and deglaze the pan, stirring with a wooden spoon to remove any browned bits from the pan bottom. Bring to a boil and boil until the liquid is reduced to 3 tablespoons, about 3 minutes.

❋ Streak warmed individual plates with the reduction and top with the veal. Serve hot.

NUTRITIONAL ANALYSIS PER SERVING: Calories 160 (Kilojoules 672); Protein 21 g; Carbohydrates 9 g; Total Fat 4 g; Saturated Fat 1 g; Cholesterol 85 mg; Sodium 613 mg; Dietary Fiber 0 g

Hoisin Chicken with Crisp Yakisoba

PREP TIME: 30 MINUTES

COOKING TIME: 30 MINUTES

INGREDIENTS

¾ lb (375 g) yakisoba noodles
  (see note)

3 cups (24 fl oz/750 ml) boiling water

2 teaspoons five-spice powder

2½ cups (10 oz/315 g) julienned leek

3 Asian (slender) eggplants
  (aubergines), thinly sliced

6 oz (185 g) fresh shiitake mushrooms, sliced

2 cups (10 oz/310 g) shredded carrots

1 lb (500 g) chicken tenders (see tip),
  thinly sliced crosswise

3 tablespoons peeled and minced
  fresh ginger

2 large cloves garlic, minced

6 tablespoons (3 fl oz/90 ml) hoisin
  sauce

½ cup (4 fl oz/125 ml) cold water

PREP TIP: Chicken tenders are cut
from the tenderloin, the leanest,
most tender portion of the breast.
Before using, strip the tendon from
the center of each tender, stroking
it with a knife to be sure it comes
out cleanly. If chicken tenders aren't
available, buy skinless, boneless
chicken breasts and cut them into
pieces ¼ inch (6 mm) thick.

Yakisoba are fresh Japanese wheat noodles that are a bit thicker
than vermicelli. Look for them in the refrigerator cases in Asian
markets and well-stocked food stores. Garnish with chopped
green (spring) onion tops for a splash of color.

SERVES 4

❀ Place the noodles in a large bowl and pour the boiling water over
them. Let stand for 5 minutes, then drain and pat dry. Toss the noodles
with 1 teaspoon of the five-spice powder.

❀ Heat a 14-inch (35-cm) nonstick frying pan over medium-high heat.
Coat the pan with nonstick cooking spray. Add the noodles, forming
them into a cake that covers the bottom of the pan. Cook until browned
on the first side, about 6 minutes. Turn over the noodle cake and cook
until browned and crispy on the second side, about 6 minutes longer.
Slide the noodle cake out of the pan onto a work surface. Cut into 4 equal
wedges and keep warm.

❀ Return the pan to the heat and coat once again with nonstick cooking
spray. Add the leek, eggplants, mushrooms, carrots, and the remaining
1 teaspoon five-spice powder. Toss and stir until the vegetables are just
beginning to soften, about 10 minutes.

❀ Add the chicken, ginger, and garlic, cover, and cook until the chicken
is opaque throughout, about 3 minutes. Add the hoisin sauce and cold
water and toss and stir until all the ingredients are well coated, about
1 minute longer.

❀ Divide the chicken mixture evenly among warmed plates and top
with the noodle wedges. Serve hot.

NUTRITIONAL ANALYSIS PER SERVING: Calories 595 (Kilojoules 2499); Protein 42 g;
Carbohydrates 103 g; Total Fat 3 g; Saturated Fat 1 g; Cholesterol 66 mg; Sodium 1260 mg;
Dietary Fiber 9 g

Saffron Orzo with Shrimp and Sugar Snap Peas

PREP TIME: 20 MINUTES

COOKING TIME: 20 MINUTES

INGREDIENTS

½ yellow onion, chopped

2 large cloves garlic, minced

2 teaspoons olive oil

1 teaspoon saffron threads

1⅓ cups (9½ oz/295 g) orzo

2¼ cups (18 fl oz/560 ml) low-sodium chicken broth

½ lb (250 g) asparagus, stems removed and cut into 1-inch (2.5-cm) pieces

½ lb (250 g) sugar snap peas, trimmed

½ lb (250 g) shrimp (prawns), peeled, deveined, and cut cross-wise into thirds

salt and ground pepper to taste

PREP TIP: You could substitute bay scallops or chunks of boneless, skinless chicken breasts for the shrimp, if you like.

Although this delicious and colorful one-pot meal is quick to make, it is fancy enough for entertaining.

SERVES 4

⊛ Heat a large saucepan over medium heat. Add the onion, garlic, olive oil, and saffron threads and sauté until soft, about 5 minutes. Mix in the orzo, then pour in the broth. Bring to a boil, cover, reduce the heat to low, and cook, stirring occasionally, until the orzo is just tender, about 8 minutes.

⊛ Add the asparagus and peas and simmer until partially cooked, about 3 minutes. Add the shrimp and cook until opaque, about 4 minutes. Season with salt and pepper. Transfer to warmed serving bowls and serve hot.

NUTRITIONAL ANALYSIS PER SERVING: Calories 315 (Kilojoules 1323); Protein 21 g; Carbohydrates 47 g; Total Fat 5 g; Saturated Fat 1 g; Cholesterol 73 mg; Sodium 134 mg; Dietary Fiber 3 g

Chicken Paupiettes with Lemon-Tarragon Sauce

PREP TIME: 35 MINUTES

COOKING TIME: 20 MINUTES

INGREDIENTS

12 large spinach leaves

1 carrot, peeled and julienned

4 skinless, boneless chicken breast
  halves, 5 oz (155 g) each

salt and ground pepper to taste

2 oz (60 g) thinly sliced prosciutto,
  trimmed

1 cup (8 fl oz/250 ml) chicken broth

1 large shallot, chopped

2 teaspoons arrowroot

2 tablespoons lemon juice

2 tablespoons fromage blanc

2 teaspoons chopped fresh tarragon,
  plus leaves for garnish

A paupiette is a thin piece of beef, chicken, or veal that is stuffed and rolled before cooking. When this particular version is sliced, it reveals a colorful pinwheel design of vegetables and meat.

SERVES 4

✤ Bring a saucepan three-fourths full of water to a boil. Add the spinach leaves and blanch for 5 seconds. Using a slotted spoon, transfer them to a plate, arranging them so that they may be easily separated; set aside. Add the carrot to the same boiling water and blanch for 2 minutes. Drain and set aside.

✤ Using a meat pounder, pound each of the chicken breasts between 2 sheets of plastic wrap to a uniform thickness of about ¼ inch (6 mm). Season the breasts with salt and pepper. Place the chicken breasts on a work surface. Arrange 3 spinach leaves atop each breast, covering the meat completely. Top the spinach with the prosciutto and then the carrot, again dividing evenly and leaving a ½-inch (12-mm) border on each of the 2 short ends of the chicken. Fold the short sides in over the filling and, beginning from a long side, roll up tightly. Tie each roll at 2-inch (5-cm) intervals with kitchen string.

✤ Heat a nonstick frying pan over medium-high heat. Coat the pan with nonstick cooking spray. Add the rolls, seam sides down, and cook until browned, about 4 minutes. Turn and continue to cook until the chicken is opaque throughout, about 4 minutes longer. Transfer the rolls to a cutting board and let rest for 8–10 minutes.

✤ Meanwhile, in a small saucepan, combine the broth and shallot and bring to a boil over high heat. Boil for about 5 minutes. In a small bowl, stir together the arrowroot and lemon juice until the arrowroot is dissolved, then whisk the mixture into the sauce. Boil until reduced to ⅔ cup (5 fl oz/160 ml), about 7 minutes.

✤ Remove from the heat and whisk in the fromage blanc and the chopped tarragon. Ladle the sauce onto warmed individual plates. Slice the rolls and fan over the sauce. Garnish with tarragon leaves and serve hot.

NUTRITIONAL ANALYSIS PER SERVING: Calories 222 (Kilojoules 932); Protein 39 g; Carbohydrates 5 g; Total Fat 4 g; Saturated Fat 1 g; Cholesterol 95 mg; Sodium 418 mg; Dietary Fiber 1 g

Poached Salmon with Cucumber Raita

PREP TIME: 20 MINUTES, PLUS
3 HOURS FOR CHILLING

COOKING TIME: 15 MINUTES

INGREDIENTS

2 teaspoons curry powder

6 salmon fillets, about 5 oz (155 g)
each

I large cucumber, peeled, seeded,
and chopped

I cup (4 oz/125 g) chopped red
(Spanish) onion

½ cup (4 oz/125 g) plain nonfat
yogurt

¼ cup (⅓ oz/10 g) chopped fresh
cilantro (fresh coriander)

3 tablespoons chopped fresh mint,
plus sprigs for garnish

I teaspoon ground cumin

salt and ground pepper to taste

COOKING TIP: For the most flavorful
and moist fish, poach the salmon in
hot, not boiling, water. Cooking at
too high a temperature will cause the
proteins in the fish to toughen and
the flesh to dry out.

Raita is a traditional Indian salad of vegetables and yogurt, served
as a cooling condiment alongside curries. Here it tops fillets of
poached salmon in a refreshing spring or summertime main
course. Accompany with basmati rice tossed with corn, peas,
diced tomatoes, and mint.

SERVES 6

✸ Fill a shallow, wide sauté pan three-fourths full with water and add
I teaspoon of the curry powder. Bring to a boil over high heat. Add the
salmon, turn off the heat, and let stand for 8 minutes. Turn and continue
to let stand until the salmon is opaque throughout, about 5 minutes
longer. Using a slotted spatula, transfer the salmon fillets to individual
plates. Cover and chill for 3–6 hours.

✸ Meanwhile, in a small bowl, stir together the remaining I teaspoon
curry, the cucumber, red onion, yogurt, cilantro, chopped mint, and cumin.
Season with salt and pepper. Cover and refrigerate until serving.

✸ To serve, spoon the raita over the salmon fillets, dividing it evenly.
Garnish with mint sprigs.

NUTRITIONAL ANALYSIS PER SERVING: Calories 231 (Kilojoules 970); Protein 30 g;
Carbohydrates 5 g; Total Fat 9 g; Saturated Fat 1 g; Cholesterol 78 mg; Sodium 84 mg;
Dietary Fiber 1 g

Herb-Crusted Beef Medallions with Zinfandel-Shallot Sauce

PREP TIME: 15 MINUTES

COOKING TIME: 50 MINUTES

INGREDIENTS

2 large shallots, chopped

1 cup (8 fl oz/250 ml) Zinfandel or other full-bodied red wine

2 cups (16 fl oz/500 ml) beef broth

2 tablespoons plus ½ cup (2½ oz/75 g) panko bread crumbs (see note) or other coarse dried bread crumbs

1 teaspoon unsalted butter

3 tablespoons chopped fresh flat-leaf (Italian) parsley

1 tablespoon each chopped fresh thyme and sage

1 egg white

4 filets mignons, trimmed, each 5 oz (155 g) and 1¼ inches (3 cm) thick

salt and ground pepper to taste

A rich-tasting but low-fat version of a restaurant-style dish, these beef medallions are coated with a crumb mixture made from panko, coarse dried bread crumbs used in Japanese cooking. If you like, garnish the plates with tiny bouquets of fresh parsley, thyme, and sage and serve with roasted Yukon Gold potatoes.

SERVES 4

❈ In a heavy saucepan over medium heat, combine the shallots and wine. Bring to a boil and boil until the liquid has evaporated, about 20 minutes. Add the broth and boil until reduced to ¾ cup (6 fl oz/180 ml), about 20 minutes longer. Remove from the heat and pour into a blender or food processor. Add the 2 tablespoons bread crumbs and the butter and purée to form a smooth sauce.

❈ About 10 minutes before the sauce is ready, in a small bowl, stir together the remaining ½ cup (2 oz/60 g) bread crumbs, the parsley, thyme, sage, and egg white.

❈ Heat a large frying pan over medium-high heat. Coat the pan with nonstick cooking spray. Season the beef medallions with salt and pepper and add to the pan. Sear, turning once, about 2 minutes on each side. Remove from the pan and press the herb mixture onto one side of each medallion.

❈ Again coat the pan with cooking spray and return to medium-high heat. Return the medallions to the pan, crumb sides down, and cook until golden and the meat is medium-rare, about 2 minutes.

❈ Remove from the heat. Ladle the puréed sauce onto warmed individual plates, dividing it evenly. Place the beef medallions, crumb sides up, on the sauce. Serve hot.

NUTRITIONAL ANALYSIS PER SERVING: Calories 314 (Kilojoules 1319); Protein 35 g; Carbohydrates 12 g; Total Fat 13 g; Saturated Fat 5 g; Cholesterol 90 mg; Sodium 182 mg; Dietary Fiber 1 g

Asian Tuna Burgers with Wasabi Mayonnaise

PREP TIME: 20 MINUTES

COOKING TIME: 5 MINUTES

INGREDIENTS

1 small English (hothouse) cucumber

1 lb (500 g) ahi tuna fillet, chopped

3 green (spring) onions, chopped

2 tablespoons peeled and minced
   fresh ginger

1 extra-large egg white

salt and ground pepper to taste

3 tablespoons fat-free mayonnaise

3 tablespoons chopped pickled ginger
   (see tip)

1½ teaspoons prepared wasabi
   (see tip)

4 sesame bagels, halved and toasted

1 package (3½ oz/105 g) daikon
   sprouts

PREP TIP: Buy the pink, sweet sliced
ginger served with sushi and found in
the refrigerated section of the super-
market, rather than the red, salty
version. If you cannot find prepared
wasabi (Japanese horseradish) in a
tube, buy powdered wasabi and use
2 tablespoons mixed with 1 tablespoon
tepid water to form a thick paste.

Asian flavors give this classy tuna burger a sprightly edge. To lighten
the sandwich further, slice each bagel horizontally into thirds
instead of halves and reserve the center slice for another use.

SERVES 4

❊ Using a vegetable peeler, shave off lengthwise slices of the cucumber
into thin ribbons. Set aside. In a bowl, combine the tuna, green onions,
fresh ginger, and egg white. Season with salt and pepper. Using your
hands, shape the tuna into 4 patties, each 4 inches (10 cm) in diameter.

❊ In a small bowl, whisk together the mayonnaise, pickled ginger, and
wasabi. Spread the mayonnaise mixture onto the cut sides of the bagels.

❊ Heat a large nonstick frying pan over medium-high heat. Coat the
pan with nonstick cooking spray. Add the patties to the pan and cook
until golden on the first side, about 2 minutes. Turn and continue to
cook until golden on the second side and medium-rare in the center,
about 2 minutes longer.

❊ Using a spatula, place a patty on the bottom slice of each bagel. Top
with the cucumber ribbons and some of the sprouts, dividing them
evenly. Divide the remaining sprouts among the bagel tops, sticking
them into the holes. Place atop the burgers and serve at once.

NUTRITIONAL ANALYSIS PER SERVING: Calories 376 (Kilojoules 1579); Protein 36 g;
Carbohydrates 48 g; Total Fat 3 g; Saturated Fat 1 g; Cholesterol 51 mg; Sodium 569 mg;
Dietary Fiber 2 g

Big Island Poke

PREP TIME: 25 MINUTES

COOKING TIME: 10 MINUTES

INGREDIENTS

¼ cup (2 fl oz/60 ml) soy sauce

¼ cup (1¼ oz/37 g) peeled and minced fresh ginger

2 tablespoons minced garlic

½ teaspoon red pepper flakes

2 teaspoons Asian sesame oil

1 lb (500 g) ahi tuna fillet, cut into 1-inch (2.5-cm) cubes

1 small yellow onion, cut into 1-inch (2.5-cm) cubes

1 red bell pepper (capsicum), seeded and cut into 1-inch (2.5-cm) pieces

½ lb (250 g) baby bok choy, coarsely chopped

5 oz (155 g) snow peas (mangetouts), trimmed and halved on the diagonal

Poke is a Hawaiian dish of marinated fish that is usually combined with seaweed. Arame, a dried, subtly flavored black seaweed available at most health-food stores, can be used here: reconstitute 2 handfuls arame in warm water for about 5 minutes, drain well, and scatter over the top as a garnish. Serve with steamed jasmine rice, if desired.

SERVES 4

✻ In a bowl, combine the soy sauce, ginger, garlic, red pepper flakes, and 1 teaspoon of the sesame oil. Stir well, then divide the mixture evenly between 2 bowls. Add the tuna to 1 bowl and toss to coat well. Reserve the other half. Cover the fish and let stand at room temperature for 20 minutes.

✻ Heat a large nonstick frying pan over high heat. Add the remaining 1 teaspoon oil and coat the pan with nonstick cooking spray. Add the onion and bell pepper and toss and stir until softened, about 4 minutes. Add the bok choy and snow peas and toss and stir until tender, about 2 minutes. Stir in the reserved soy mixture and cook for 1 minute.

✻ Push the vegetables to the far side of the pan, and add the tuna and its marinade to the empty part of the pan. Toss and stir until the tuna is opaque but still pink at the center, about 2 minutes.

✻ Remove from the heat and transfer the tuna and vegetables to a warmed serving platter and serve hot.

NUTRITIONAL ANALYSIS PER SERVING: Calories 206 (Kilojoules 865); Protein 30 g; Carbohydrates 12 g; Total Fat 4 g; Saturated Fat 1 g; Cholesterol 51 mg; Sodium 1112 mg; Dietary Fiber 2 g

Mushroom Ravioli in Spring Vegetable Stock

PREP TIME: 30 MINUTES

COOKING TIME: 10 MINUTES

INGREDIENTS

¼ cup (1 oz/30 g) chopped shallots

¼ lb (125 g) fresh shiitake mushrooms, chopped

¼ lb (125 g) fresh oyster mushrooms, chopped

¾ teaspoon dried thyme

salt and ground pepper to taste

3 tablespoons basil-flavored fresh goat cheese

4 tablespoons (⅓ oz/10 g) snipped fresh chives

16 gyoza wrappers

4 cups (32 fl oz/1 l) Spring Vegetable Stock (page 13) or broth

16 asparagus tips

1 package (3½ oz/105 g) enoki mushrooms, trimmed

Here, gyoza wrappers, small dough rounds traditionally used for making Japanese dumplings, take the place of pasta. Serve these ravioli as the opening course to a special-occasion alfresco dinner or as a lunch main dish, accompanied by a fresh-from-the-garden salad.

SERVES 4

❊ Heat a nonstick frying pan over medium heat. Coat the pan with nonstick cooking spray. Add the shallots and sauté until softened, about 3 minutes. Add the shiitakes and sauté for about 2 minutes. Stir in the oyster mushrooms and thyme and season with salt and pepper. Sauté until the mushrooms are golden, about 3 minutes longer. Transfer to a bowl and stir in the cheese and 2 tablespoons of the chives. Let cool.

❊ Place the gyoza wrappers on a work surface and divide the mushroom mixture evenly among them, positioning a mound in the center of each wrapper. Moisten the edges of each wrapper with water and fold in half to create a half-moon. Pinch the edges together to seal well.

❊ In a large, shallow saucepan, bring the stock or broth to a simmer over medium heat. Add half of the ravioli and asparagus to the stock and cook, uncovered, turning the ravioli once, until they are just tender, about 1½ minutes.

❊ Using a slotted spoon, divide the ravioli and asparagus among warmed soup bowls. Repeat with the remaining ravioli and asparagus.

❊ Ladle the stock or broth over the ravioli. Garnish each bowl with the enoki mushrooms and the remaining 2 tablespoons chives, dividing them evenly. Serve immediately.

NUTRITIONAL ANALYSIS PER SERVING: Calories 158 (Kilojoules 664); Protein 8 g; Carbohydrates 26 g; Total Fat 3 g; Saturated Fat 2 g; Cholesterol 14 mg; Sodium 245 mg; Dietary Fiber 2 g

Lemon-Thyme Polenta and Roasted Mediterranean Vegetables

PREP TIME: 30 MINUTES, PLUS
5½ HOURS FOR MARINATING
AND CHILLING

COOKING TIME: 45 MINUTES

INGREDIENTS

2¾ cups (22 fl oz/680 ml) Spring Vegetable Stock *(page 13)* or chicken broth

1 cup (5 oz/155 g) yellow cornmeal

1 tablespoon plus 4 teaspoons chopped garlic

4 teaspoons chopped fresh lemon thyme

salt and ground pepper to taste

¼ cup (2 fl oz/60 ml) balsamic vinegar

2 tablespoons drained and minced oil-packed sun-dried tomatoes

5 Asian (slender) eggplants (aubergines), halved lengthwise and cut crosswise into 1-inch (2.5-cm) pieces

3 zucchini (courgettes), cut into slices 1 inch (2.5 cm) thick

8 small red potatoes, quartered

1 large red bell pepper (capsicum), seeded and cut into 1-inch (2.5-cm) pieces

2 red (Spanish) onions, each cut into eighths

You can prepare the polenta up to 2 days in advance, if desired. Regular thyme may be substituted for the lemon thyme, although it won't have the same citrusy fragrance.

SERVES 6

❀ Line an 8½-by-4½-inch (21.5-by-11.5-cm) loaf pan with plastic wrap.

❀ In a saucepan over medium heat, whisk together 2½ cups (20 fl oz/ 625 ml) of the stock or broth, the cornmeal, 1 tablespoon of the garlic, and 2 teaspoons of the thyme. Continue to whisk until the cornmeal is thick and smooth, about 12 minutes. Season liberally with salt and pepper. Pour the cornmeal into the prepared pan, spreading it evenly and smoothing the top. Let cool, cover, and chill until firm, at least 5 hours.

❀ Preheat an oven to 400°F (200°C).

❀ In a large bowl, combine the remaining ¼ cup (2 fl oz/60 ml) stock or broth, the vinegar, sun-dried tomatoes, and the remaining 4 teaspoons garlic and 2 teaspoons thyme. Add the eggplants, zucchini, potatoes, and bell pepper. Toss well and let stand for 20 minutes.

❀ Coat 3 baking sheets with nonstick cooking spray. Turn out the polenta onto a cutting board, and cut into 12 equal slices. Place the polenta slices in a single layer on the prepared baking sheet. Arrange the marinated vegetables and onions on the other 2 baking sheets. Season with salt and pepper.

❀ Place all 3 baking sheets in the oven and roast for 15 minutes. Turn over the vegetables and polenta and continue to roast until browned, about 10 minutes longer for the vegetables and 15 minutes longer for the polenta.

❀ Transfer the vegetables to warmed individual plates, dividing them evenly. Garnish each plate with 2 polenta slices. Serve at once.

NUTRITIONAL ANALYSIS PER SERVING: Calories 303 (Kilojoules 1273); Protein 9 g; Carbohydrates 65 g; Total Fat 2 g; Saturated Fat 0 g; Cholesterol 0 mg; Sodium 52 mg; Dietary Fiber 8 g

Petrale Napoleons with Ratatouille Confit

PREP TIME: 35 MINUTES

COOKING TIME: 35 MINUTES

INGREDIENTS

1 eggplant (aubergine), ½ lb (250 g), unpeeled, cut into ½-inch (12-mm) dice

1 small yellow onion, chopped

2 teaspoons herbes de Provence

1 yellow bell pepper (capsicum), seeded and cut into ½-inch (12-mm) dice

2 teaspoons sugar

salt and ground pepper to taste

4 large plum (Roma) tomatoes, seeded and diced

3 large cloves garlic, minced

2 tablespoons tomato paste

3 tablespoons each chopped fresh basil and flat-leaf (Italian) parsley

½ cup (4 fl oz/125 ml) chicken broth

4 petrale or lemon sole fillets, about 5 oz (155 g) each

1 teaspoon olive oil

Here, sole fillets are layered with ratatouille, then more ratatouille is puréed to make a sauce. The ratatouille can be prepared 2–3 days ahead. Sautéed spinach is a good accompaniment.

SERVES 4

❋ Heat a large nonstick frying pan over medium heat. Coat the pan with nonstick cooking spray. Add the eggplant, onion, and herbes de Provence and sauté until just tender, about 15 minutes. Push the vegetables to one side and coat the pan again with nonstick cooking spray. Add the bell pepper and stir to combine with the vegetables in the pan. Season with sugar, salt, and pepper and continue cooking until the bell pepper is tender, about 8 minutes longer. Stir in the tomatoes and garlic and sauté until softened, about 3 minutes. Mix in the tomato paste, cover, and cook until the vegetables are soft, about 5 minutes longer. Remove from the heat and let cool. Stir in 1 tablespoon each of the basil and parsley, and taste and adjust the seasonings.

❋ In a blender, combine ¾ cup (6 oz/185 g) of the eggplant mixture and the broth. Blend until smooth. Transfer the sauce to a saucepan. Place the remaining eggplant mixture in another saucepan.

❋ In a small bowl, combine the remaining 2 tablespoons each basil and parsley. Season the sole fillets with salt and pepper. Press the herbs onto 1 side of each fillet. Heat a large nonstick frying pan over medium-high heat. Coat the pan with nonstick cooking spray. Add the fillets, herb sides down, and cook until golden, 2 minutes. Turn and continue to cook until the fillets feel firm, about 1 minute longer. Remove from the heat.

❋ Meanwhile, place the saucepans holding the sauce and the ratatouille over low heat, and reheat gently. Stir the olive oil into the sauce and season with salt and pepper.

❋ The fillets will separate in half at their natural seam. Place one-half of each fillet on an individual warmed plate. Top each fillet half with one-fourth of the ratatouille. Top with the second half of each fillet. Spoon the sauce around the stacked fish. Serve hot.

NUTRITIONAL ANALYSIS PER SERVING: Calories 212 (Kilojoules 890); Protein 29 g; Carbohydrates 15 g; Total Fat 4 g; Saturated Fat 1 g; Cholesterol 69 mg; Sodium 203 mg; Dietary Fiber 3 g

Penne with White Beans, Arugula, and Pecorino

PREP TIME: 20 MINUTES

COOKING TIME: 15 MINUTES

INGREDIENTS

¾ lb (375 g) penne

½ red (Spanish) onion, chopped

½ teaspoon red pepper flakes

3 large cloves garlic, chopped

1 can (15 oz/470 g) cannellini beans, undrained

2 oz (60 g) arugula (rocket) leaves, torn

½ lb (250 g) smoked chicken meat, cubed

5 tablespoons grated pecorino cheese

salt and ground pepper to taste

PREP TIP: Not all dried pastas are created equal. For the best texture, look for pastas that are made from 100 percent durum wheat (or semolina).

Prepare this stick-to-your-ribs pasta dish for a quick and satisfying lunch or casual supper. Farfalle (bow tie) or rotelle (corkscrew) pasta would work well, too.

SERVES 4

❀ Bring a large pot three-fourths full of salted water to a boil over high heat. Add the penne, stir well, and cook until al dente (tender but firm to the bite), about 15 minutes or according to the package directions.

❀ Meanwhile, heat a large nonstick frying pan over medium heat. Coat the pan with nonstick cooking spray. Add the onion and red pepper flakes and sauté until soft, about 5 minutes. Add the garlic and the beans with their liquid and cook, stirring constantly, until the beans are heated through, about 1½ minutes. Add the arugula and continue to cook, stirring, until wilted, about 1 minute.

❀ Drain the pasta and add to the frying pan along with the smoked chicken. Stir for about 30 seconds to warm the chicken. Sprinkle with the cheese and season with salt and pepper. Mix well.

❀ Divide among warmed serving bowls and serve hot.

NUTRITIONAL ANALYSIS PER SERVING: Calories 524 (Kilojoules 2201); Protein 27 g; Carbohydrates 83 g; Total Fat 9 g; Saturated Fat 3 g; Cholesterol 41 mg; Sodium 596 mg; Dietary Fiber 7 g

Pork Chops with Roasted Shallot, Tomato, and Rosemary Relish

PREP TIME: 15 MINUTES

COOKING TIME: 35 MINUTES

INGREDIENTS

6 large shallots, halved

salt and ground black pepper to taste

4 plum (Roma) tomatoes, seeded
   and chopped

¼ cup (⅓ oz/10 g) chopped fresh
   flat-leaf (Italian) parsley

1 tablespoon balsamic vinegar

1 tablespoon honey

2 teaspoons minced fresh rosemary,
   plus sprigs for garnish

¼ teaspoon cayenne pepper

4 boneless pork loin chops, 5 oz
   (155 g) each, trimmed of fat

PREP TIP: For a prettier colored relish, use white balsamic vinegar, which may be found in some specialty-food stores and Italian delicatessens.

The relish improves in flavor if made 2 or 3 days before serving. You might even make a double batch and keep the second one on hand for a night when you don't feel like cooking.

SERVES 4

❋ Preheat an oven to 400°F (200°C).

❋ Place the shallots in a baking pan. Season with salt and pepper, and coat with nonstick cooking spray. Roast for 15 minutes. Turn over the shallots and continue to roast until soft, about 10 minutes longer. Remove from the oven, let cool, and chop coarsely.

❋ In a bowl, combine the shallots, tomatoes, parsley, vinegar, honey, minced rosemary, and cayenne. Season to taste with salt and pepper. Set aside, or cover and refrigerate for up to 3 days.

❋ Heat a large frying pan over medium-high heat. Coat the pan with nonstick cooking spray. Season the pork chops with salt and black pepper. Add the chops to the pan and cook on the first side until well seared, about 4 minutes. Turn and continue to cook until pale pink when cut into at the thickest point, about 3 minutes longer.

❋ Transfer the pork chops to a warmed platter and top with the relish, dividing evenly. Garnish with rosemary sprigs and serve hot.

NUTRITIONAL ANALYSIS PER SERVING: Calories 185 (Kilojoules 777); Protein 22 g; Carbohydrates 10 g; Total Fat 6 g; Saturated Fat 2 g; Cholesterol 59 mg; Sodium 59 mg; Dietary Fiber 1 g

Turkey with Curried Apricot Glaze

PREP TIME: 15 MINUTES

COOKING TIME: 15 MINUTES

INGREDIENTS

¼ cup (2½ oz/75 g) apricot preserves

2 tablespoons white wine vinegar

2½ teaspoons Dijon mustard

2½ teaspoons curry powder

1 teaspoon minced garlic

3 fat-free (99%) turkey tenderloins,
   ½ lb (250 g) each

salt and ground pepper to taste

1½ tablespoons dried cranberries

COOKING TIP: If turkey tenderloins
are unavailable, use two 3-ounce
(90-g) boneless turkey breast cutlets
per serving. Sauté over medium heat
for 2 minutes, then turn and cook for
1 minute longer. Reduce the broiling
time to 2 minutes total.

Accompany this festive holiday offering with wild rice tossed with corn and green (spring) onions. Dried cherries can be substituted for the cranberries in the glaze.

SERVES 4

❋ In a small bowl, combine the apricot preserves, vinegar, mustard, curry, and garlic. Stir to mix well and set aside.

❋ Preheat a broiler (griller). Heat a large frying pan over medium heat. Coat the pan with nonstick cooking spray. Season the turkey with salt and pepper and add it to the pan. Cook the turkey until browned, about 5 minutes. Turn the turkey over and cover the pan. Cook until just opaque throughout, about 5 minutes longer. Remove from the heat.

❋ Arrange the turkey tenderloins on a baking sheet. Spoon 1 tablespoon of the apricot mixture over each tenderloin. Slip under the broiler about 4 inches (10 cm) from the heat source and broil for 2 minutes. Mix the cranberries into the remaining apricot mixture and spoon over the turkey, dividing it evenly. Continue to broil until the turkey is well glazed, about 2 minutes longer.

❋ Transfer the turkey tenderloins to a work surface. Let rest for 7 minutes. Slice the turkey on the diagonal and divide among warmed individual plates, fanning the slices. Serve hot.

NUTRITIONAL ANALYSIS PER SERVING: Calories 252 (Kilojoules 1058); Protein 42 g; Carbohydrates 15 g; Total Fat 2 g; Saturated Fat 0 g; Cholesterol 106 mg; Sodium 166 mg; Dietary Fiber 1 g

Seared Scallops with Tropical Salsa

PREP TIME: 20 MINUTES

COOKING TIME: 10 MINUTES

INGREDIENTS

½ cup (3 oz/90 g) diced pineapple

½ cup (3 oz/90 g) diced mango

½ cup (2½ oz/75 g) diced cucumber

½ cup (2½ oz/75 g) diced red bell pepper (capsicum)

3 tablespoons chopped fresh cilantro (fresh coriander)

4 teaspoons fresh lime juice

1 jalapeño chile, seeded and minced

salt and ground pepper to taste

16 sea scallops, about 1 lb (500 g) total weight

PREP TIP: To remove the flesh of a mango, score the skin lengthwise into quarters and peel it off, then cut off the flesh into thick slices from either side of the large, flat pit. Trim the remaining fruit from around the pit's edges.

Feel free to substitute any of your favorite exotic fruits for the pineapple and mango in the salsa. Be sure to use the large, plump sea scallop rather than the small bay scallop when preparing this dish. Take care not to overcook the scallops, which can toughen if exposed to heat for too long. When properly cooked, the scallops will remain tender and moist.

SERVES 4

❊ In a bowl, combine the pineapple, mango, cucumber, bell pepper, cilantro, lime juice, and chile. Toss well to form a salsa. Season to taste with salt and pepper. Set aside.

❊ Heat a large nonstick frying pan over medium-high heat. Coat the pan with nonstick cooking spray. Season the scallops with salt and pepper. Add half of the scallops to the pan and sear, turning once, until golden brown on both sides and opaque throughout, about 2 minutes on each side. Transfer the scallops to a warmed plate. Keep warm while cooking the remaining scallops in the same way.

❊ Divide the scallops among warmed individual plates. Spoon the salsa over the tops, dividing it evenly. Serve immediately.

NUTRITIONAL ANALYSIS PER SERVING: Calories 136 (Kilojoules 571); Protein 20 g; Carbohydrates 11 g; Total Fat 1 g; Saturated Fat 0 g; Cholesterol 37 mg; Sodium 185 mg; Dietary Fiber 1 g

Grilled Chipotle-Marinated Pork

PREP TIME: 15 MINUTES,
PLUS 4 HOURS FOR
MARINATING

COOKING TIME: 10 MINUTES,
PLUS PREPARING FIRE

INGREDIENTS

2 pork tenderloins, 10 oz (315 g) each, trimmed of fat

3 canned chipotle chiles in adobo sauce, seeded

2 tablespoons lime juice

3 tablespoons honey

2 large cloves garlic

1 tablespoon soy sauce

2 teaspoons ground cumin

¼ cup (⅓ oz/10 g) chopped fresh cilantro (fresh coriander), plus sprigs for garnish

COOKING TIP: If canned chipotle chiles are unavailable, reconstitute 3 dried chipotles in hot water until softened, 10–15 minutes. Drain, stem, and seed the chiles before puréeing with the glaze ingredients.

The slightly sweet-and-hot glaze gives this pork a full, delicious flavor. Be sure not to overcook the pork or it will become tough and dry. Pork today can be safely eaten when it is still pale pink inside.

SERVES 4

❂ Cut each tenderloin in half crosswise. Set aside. In a blender, combine the chipotle chiles, lime juice, honey, garlic, soy sauce, and cumin. Blend until smooth. Stir in the cilantro. Transfer half of the mixture to a shallow, nonaluminum bowl. Reserve the other half. Add the pork to the bowl and turn to coat. Cover and refrigerate for 4–6 hours.

❂ Prepare a fire in a grill, or preheat a griddle over medium-high heat.

❂ Coat the grill rack or griddle surface with nonstick cooking spray. Remove the pork from the marinade and place on the grill rack about 6–8 inches (15–20 cm) from the fire or on the griddle. Cook until seared on the first side, about 4 minutes. Turn over the pork and spoon the reserved chile mixture evenly on top of the pieces. Tent them with aluminum foil. Continue to cook until the pork is just firm to the touch and pale pink when cut into at the thickest point, about 4 minutes longer.

❂ Transfer to a cutting board and let rest for about 7 minutes. Slice and arrange on warmed individual plates. Garnish with cilantro sprigs and serve hot.

NUTRITIONAL ANALYSIS PER SERVING: Calories 242 (Kilojoules 1016); Protein 28 g; Carbohydrates 17 g; Total Fat 6 g; Saturated Fat 2 g; Cholesterol 86 mg; Sodium 416 mg; Dietary Fiber 1 g

Moroccan-Spiced Vegetarian Chili

PREP TIME: 30 MINUTES

COOKING TIME: 45 MINUTES

INGREDIENTS

4 large ancho chiles

3 cups (24 fl oz/750 ml) water

4 large whole cloves garlic, plus
6 large cloves, sliced

1 yellow onion, chopped

1½ teaspoons each of ground
turmeric, cinnamon, cumin, and
coriander

1 can (28 oz/875 g) chopped
tomatoes

1 butternut squash, 1¼ lb (625 g),
halved, seeded, peeled, and cut
into ½-inch (12-mm) cubes

2 cans (15½ oz/485 g each) chickpeas (garbanzo beans)

2 zucchini (courgettes), cut into
½-inch (12-mm) dice

⅓ cup (2 oz/60 g) sliced dried
apricots

⅓ cup (2 oz/60 g) sliced pitted
prunes

Serve this richly spiced vegetarian chili with toasted pita points or on a bed of steamed couscous or rice. Other winter squashes such as Hubbard or acorn may be used in place of the butternut squash.

SERVES 6

❊ In a saucepan, combine the chiles and water and bring to a boil. Remove from the heat. Cover and let stand for 15 minutes. Using tongs or a slotted spoon, transfer the chiles to a work surface; reserve the liquid. Discard the stems and seeds from the chiles. In a blender or food processor, combine the chiles with the 4 cloves garlic and ½ cup (4 fl oz/125 ml) of the liquid. Process until smooth. Set aside.

❊ Heat a heavy pot over medium heat. Coat the pan with nonstick cooking spray. Add the onion, the sliced garlic cloves, turmeric, cinnamon, cumin, and coriander and sauté until the onion and garlic have softened, about 5 minutes. Stir in the tomatoes and their juices, butternut squash, and the chile purée. Cover and simmer, stirring occasionally, until the squash is just tender, about 25 minutes.

❊ Stir in the chickpeas with their liquid, the zucchini, and dried apricots and prunes. Simmer, uncovered, until all of the squashes are tender, about 15 minutes longer. Transfer to a warmed serving dish and serve hot.

NUTRITIONAL ANALYSIS PER SERVING: Calories 363 (Kilojoules 1525); Protein 13 g; Carbohydrates 76 g; Total Fat 5 g; Saturated Fat 1 g; Cholesterol 0 mg; Sodium 1041 mg; Dietary Fiber 10 g

Chicken Satay with Coconut-Lime Curry Sauce

PREP TIME: 20 MINUTES,
PLUS 1 HOUR FOR
MARINATING

COOKING TIME: 15 MINUTES

INGREDIENTS

16 chicken tenders, about 1¼ lb
(625 g) total weight

1 tablespoon soy sauce

2 tablespoons peeled and minced
fresh ginger

2 large cloves garlic, minced

2 teaspoons curry powder

1 cup (8 fl oz/250 ml) nonfat milk

1 tablespoon sugar

2 teaspoons arrowroot

2 teaspoons water

2 tablespoons lime juice

1 teaspoon coconut extract (essence)

salt to taste

For a little extra heat and color, garnish the curry sauce with minced red or green jalapeño chiles. Serve these on a bed of warm couscous. If chicken tenders are unavailable, cut boneless, skinless chicken breasts into strips 1 inch (2.5 cm) wide.

SERVES 4

❋ In a bowl, toss together the chicken and soy sauce. Cover and refrigerate for 1 hour. Meanwhile, soak 16 wooden skewers in warm water to cover for at least 15 minutes. Thread the chicken onto the skewers.

❋ Heat a saucepan over medium heat. Coat the pan with nonstick cooking spray. Add the ginger, garlic, and curry powder and sauté for 1 minute. Add the milk and sugar, stir well, and simmer for 5 minutes to blend the flavors.

❋ In a small bowl, stir the arrowroot into 2 teaspoons water until dissolved. Whisk it into the curry mixture and simmer until thickened, about 2 minutes. Remove the sauce from the heat and whisk in the lime juice and coconut extract. Season with salt. Keep warm.

❋ Preheat a broiler (griller). Coat a baking sheet with nonstick cooking spray. Place the skewers in a single layer on the baking sheet. Slip under the broiler about 4 inches (10 cm) from the heat source. Broil (grill), turning once, until the chicken is opaque throughout, about 3 minutes on each side.

❋ Remove from the broiler. Arrange the skewers on warmed individual plates. Spoon the sauce over them and serve hot.

NUTRITIONAL ANALYSIS PER SERVING: Calories 212 (Kilojoules 890); Protein 35 g; Carbohydrates 10 g; Total Fat 3 g; Saturated Fat 1 g; Cholesterol 84 mg; Sodium 384 mg; Dietary Fiber 0 g

Zucchini "Pasta" with Mint Pesto

PREP TIME: 20 MINUTES

COOKING TIME: 15 MINUTES

INGREDIENTS

1 cup (1½ oz/45 g) firmly packed
 fresh mint leaves

⅓ cup (3 fl oz/80 ml) Spring Vegetable
 Stock (page 13) or broth

3 tablespoons grated asiago cheese,
 plus extra for garnish, if desired

2 large cloves garlic, cut up

2 teaspoons olive oil

3 yellow summer squashes, about
 ¾ lb (375 g) total weight

3 zucchini (courgettes), about ¾ lb
 (375 g) total weight

¼ cup (1 oz/30 g) chopped shallot

1½ teaspoons dried thyme

salt and ground pepper to taste

COOKING TIP: Be careful not to overcook the squashes. If they remain on
the heat too long, they will release
too many of their natural juices.

For a dish with more dramatic contrasts of color, use only the squash flesh that includes some of the colored skin. In this case, you will need about 8 green and 8 yellow squashes.

SERVES 4–6

❀ In a blender or food processor, combine the mint, the stock or broth, 2 tablespoons of the cheese, the garlic, and the olive oil. Process until smooth. Set aside.

❀ Using a mandoline or a vegetable peeler, cut the yellow squashes and zucchini into long, narrow ribbons.

❀ Heat a large nonstick frying pan over medium heat. Coat the pan with nonstick cooking spray. Add the shallots and sauté until softened, about 3 minutes. Add the yellow squashes and zucchini and the thyme and season generously with salt and pepper. Sauté until the squashes are just tender, about 8 minutes longer.

❀ Stir in the mint pesto and heat for 1 minute. Remove from the heat and stir in the remaining 1 tablespoon cheese.

❀ Transfer to a warmed serving dish and toss with extra cheese, if you like. Serve hot.

NUTRITIONAL ANALYSIS PER SERVING: Calories 80 (Kilojoules 336); Protein 4 g; Carbohydrates 10 g; Total Fat 3 g; Saturated Fat 1 g; Cholesterol 3 mg; Sodium 58 mg; Dietary Fiber 2 g

Potato and Roasted Garlic Gratin

PREP TIME: 20 MINUTES

COOKING TIME: 3½ HOURS

INGREDIENTS

1 large head garlic, about 2 oz (60 g)

2 cups (16 fl oz/500 ml) Spring Vegetable Stock (*page 13*) or broth

2 lb (1 kg) russet potatoes, unpeeled, thinly sliced

1 large yellow onion, thinly sliced

1 tablespoon chopped fresh sage

salt and ground pepper to taste

¼ cup (1 oz/30 g) grated Parmesan cheese

3 tablespoons fresh bread crumbs

Don't bother to peel the potatoes for this quick and hearty gratin. There is a wealth of minerals contained in their skins.

SERVES 8

❋ Preheat an oven to 300°F (150°C).

❋ Wrap the unpeeled whole garlic head in aluminum foil. Bake until the cloves are very soft, about 1½ hours. Remove from the oven and set aside. Raise the oven temperature to 350°F (180°C).

❋ Squeeze the pulp from the garlic cloves into a large bowl. Gradually whisk in the stock or broth. Add the potatoes, onion, and sage and toss to coat the potato slices evenly. Press half of the potato mixture into a 7-by-11-inch (18-by-28-cm) baking dish, forming an even layer. Season generously with salt and pepper and sprinkle with 1 tablespoon of the cheese. Top with the remaining potato mixture, and press it into an even layer. Pour the liquid mixture remaining in the bowl evenly over the top. Cover the dish with aluminum foil and bake for 1 hour.

❋ In a small bowl, stir together the remaining 3 tablespoons cheese and the bread crumbs. Uncover the baking dish and sprinkle the cheese mixture evenly over the top. Continue to bake, uncovered, until the potatoes are tender and crusty, about 50 minutes. Remove from the oven and let stand for 10 minutes before serving.

NUTRITIONAL ANALYSIS PER SERVING: Calories 134 (Kilojoules 563); Protein 4 g; Carbohydrates 27 g; Total Fat 1 g; Saturated Fat 1 g; Cholesterol 2 mg; Sodium 76 mg; Dietary Fiber 3 g

Artichoke and Radicchio Barley "Risotto"

PREP TIME: 25 MINUTES

COOKING TIME: 45 MINUTES

INGREDIENTS

juice of 1 lemon

16 baby artichokes, about 1 lb (500 g) total weight

1 head radicchio, ¼ lb (125 g)

¾ cup (3 oz/90 g) chopped yellow onion

1 cup (8 oz/250 g) pearl barley

3¼ cups (26 fl oz/810 ml) Spring Vegetable Stock (page 13) or broth

2 teaspoons chopped fresh thyme, plus sprigs for garnish (optional)

2 tablespoons grated Parmesan cheese, plus extra for garnish

salt and ground pepper to taste

Cook barley as you would rice for risotto and the end result is a delicious dish with some of the same chewy-creamy characteristics as the popular Italian favorite.

SERVES 6

❋ Have ready a bowl three-fourths full of water to which you have added the lemon juice. Working with 1 artichoke at a time, pull off and discard the tough outer leaves until you reach the tender, pale yellow-green inner leaves. Cut off about 1 inch (2.5 cm) from the top to remove the prickly tips. Cut off the stem end even with the bottom. Cut the trimmed artichokes lengthwise in halves or quarters, depending upon their size. As each artichoke is finished, drop it into the lemon water.

❋ Meanwhile, bring a saucepan three-fourths full of water to a boil. Drain the artichokes and add them to the boiling water. Cook until tender when pierced with the tip of a knife, about 10 minutes. Drain well and set aside.

❋ Remove 6 of the outer leaves from the radicchio and set aside. Thinly slice enough radicchio to measure 1 cup (3 oz/90 g). Set aside.

❋ Heat a saucepan over medium heat. Coat the pan with nonstick cooking spray. Add the onion and sauté until softened, about 4 minutes. Add the barley and stir for 1 minute. Stir in 2 cups (16 fl oz/500 ml) of the stock or broth and bring to a simmer. Simmer the barley, stirring frequently, for 10 minutes. Stir in the remaining 1¼ cups (10 fl oz/310 ml) stock or broth and continue to simmer, stirring frequently, just until the barley is creamy and tender, about 15 minutes.

❋ Stir in the artichokes and chopped thyme and cook until heated through, about 2 minutes. Remove from the heat and stir in ⅔ cup (2 oz/60 g) of the radicchio and the 2 tablespoons cheese. Season with salt and pepper.

❋ Place the reserved radicchio leaves in 6 individual bowls. Divide the barley evenly among the bowls. Sprinkle with the remaining ⅓ cup (1 oz/30 g) radicchio and a little Parmesan cheese, dividing evenly. Garnish with thyme sprigs, if using. Serve immediately.

NUTRITIONAL ANALYSIS PER SERVING: Calories 187 (Kilojoules 785); Protein 7 g; Carbohydrates 39 g; Total Fat 1 g; Saturated Fat 0 g; Cholesterol 2 mg; Sodium 95 mg; Dietary Fiber 9 g

"Creamy" Tex-Mex Corn with Lime

PREP TIME: 10 MINUTES

COOKING TIME: 10 MINUTES

INGREDIENTS

3 cups (18 oz/560 g) corn kernels

I large shallot, chopped

I clove garlic, chopped

I teaspoon ground cumin

I teaspoon chili powder

I cup (8 fl oz/250 ml) nonfat milk

2 tablespoons fresh goat cheese

1½ teaspoons minced lime zest

¼ cup (⅓ oz/10 g) snipped fresh
    chives

salt and ground pepper to taste

PREP TIP: To remove kernels from
an ear of corn, stand the ear on its
stem end and, using a knife, cut down
its length to remove the kernels.
Rotate the corn about one-quarter,
and cut again. Repeat until all the
kernels are removed.

This exceedingly simple and very adaptable dish is spiked with lime, cumin, and chili powder, but it can be flavored to fit many cuisines by altering the seasonings. For an Indian accent, use curry powder, lemon zest, and cilantro in place of the chili powder, lime, and chives. Or substitute a generous pinch of herbes de Provence to give the dish a Provençal flavor.

SERVES 4

❊ Heat a large nonstick frying pan over medium heat. Coat the pan with nonstick cooking spray. Add the corn, shallot, garlic, cumin, and chili powder and sauté until the corn starts to soften, about 4 minutes.

❊ Stir in the milk and cheese and simmer, uncovered, until the liquid thickens, about 4 minutes. Mix in the lime zest and chives and season with salt and pepper.

❊ Transfer to a warmed serving bowl and serve immediately.

NUTRITIONAL ANALYSIS PER SERVING: Calories 152 (Kilojoules 638); Protein 7 g; Carbohydrates 29 g; Total Fat 3 g; Saturated Fat 1 g; Cholesterol 3 mg; Sodium 75 mg; Dietary Fiber 4 g

Cheese-Herb Hominy Grits

PREP TIME: 10 MINUTES

COOKING TIME: 20 MINUTES

INGREDIENTS

2 teaspoons corn oil

½ small yellow onion, chopped

¾ cup (4½ oz/140 g) quick-cooking
  hominy grits

2 cups (16 fl oz/500 ml) chicken broth

salt and ground pepper to taste

¼ cup (2 fl oz/60 ml) low-fat
  buttermilk

2 tablespoons fresh goat cheese

2 tablespoons snipped fresh chives

2 tablespoons chopped fresh basil

COOKING TIP: For a thicker mixture,
use only 1¼ cups (10 fl oz/310 ml)
broth. Pour the fully cooked grits
into an oiled loaf pan, let cool, cover,
and chill until set. Turn out of the
pan and cut into slices. Sauté or grill
as you would for polenta.

Robust in flavor and texture yet light in fat, these grits make a
great accompaniment to hearty main courses. You can use this
same recipe to make a soft-style polenta by substituting cornmeal
for the grits. Cook the polenta until it pulls away from the sides
of the pot, about 20 minutes.

SERVES 4

❉ In a saucepan over medium heat, warm the corn oil. Add the onion
and sauté until soft, about 5 minutes. Stir in the grits and then whisk in
the broth. Season with salt and pepper. Simmer uncovered, whisking
occasionally, until the grits are thick and translucent, about 10 minutes.

❉ Whisk in the buttermilk and cook until incorporated, about 2 minutes longer. Whisk in the cheese, chives, and basil. Taste and adjust the
seasonings. Transfer to a warmed serving dish and serve immediately.

NUTRITIONAL ANALYSIS PER SERVING: Calories 176 (Kilojoules 739); Protein 6 g;
Carbohydrates 28 g; Total Fat 5 g; Saturated Fat 2 g; Cholesterol 6 mg; Sodium 97 mg;
Dietary Fiber 2 g

Fava Beans with Pancetta and Lemon

PREP TIME: 25 MINUTES

COOKING TIME: 15 MINUTES

INGREDIENTS

2¼ lb (1.1 kg) fava (broad) beans, shelled

2 thin slices pancetta, chopped

1 large carrot, peeled and thinly sliced

1½ teaspoons minced lemon zest

1 teaspoon chopped fresh sage

salt and ground pepper to taste

Fava beans grow inside thick pods and have a rich, buttery flavor. Shell them as you would peas by first snapping off the stem and pulling away the tough string on the side of the pod. Then pop each pod open by pressing your thumbnails along its seam. This dish is a lovely accompaniment to herbed veal or lamb chops.

SERVES 4

❀ Bring a saucepan three-fourths full of water to a boil. Add the fava beans and cook for 3 minutes. Drain the beans. When cool enough to handle, split the translucent skin covering each bean and pop the bean free of the skin. Set the beans aside.

❀ In a heavy frying pan over medium heat, sauté the pancetta until crisp, about 3 minutes. Add the carrot and sauté until tender, about 5 minutes.

❀ Stir in the fava beans, lemon zest, and sage, mixing well. Season with salt and pepper. Transfer to a warmed serving dish and serve hot.

NUTRITIONAL ANALYSIS PER SERVING: Calories 100 (Kilojoules 420); Protein 6 g; Carbohydrates 13 g; Total Fat 3 g; Saturated Fat 1 g; Cholesterol 4 mg; Sodium 127 mg; Dietary Fiber 4 g

Pears Poached in Sauternes with Vanilla Bean

PREP TIME: 20 MINUTES

COOKING TIME: 1 HOUR

INGREDIENTS

1¾ cups (14 fl oz/430 ml) Sauternes wine

1 cup (8 fl oz/250 ml) water

⅓ cup (3 oz/90 g) sugar

2 teaspoons lemon juice

1 vanilla bean, split lengthwise

4 small, firm yet ripe pears such as Bosc

1½ cups (6 oz/185 g) frozen raspberries, thawed

1 pint (16 fl oz/500 ml) fat-free vanilla frozen yogurt

1½ cups (6 oz/185 g) fresh raspberries

fresh mint sprigs

PREP TIP: Scrape the seeds from the inside of the vanilla bean with the tip of a paring knife.

Any Sauternes, Beaumes de Venise, or other dessert wine will work well in this recipe. The wine is used to poach the pears and to make the sauce. Refrigerate the remaining sauce, covered, for up to 1 week. Serve it on top of frozen yogurt or with fresh, mixed berries.

SERVES 4

✹ In a wide, shallow pan over medium heat, combine the wine, water, sugar, and lemon juice. Scrape the seeds from the vanilla bean into the wine mixture, then add the pod halves as well. Stir until the sugar dissolves, about 2 minutes.

✹ Peel the pears. Using an apple corer, and starting at the blossom end, core each pear, stopping just short of the stem so that it remains intact. Add the pears to the simmering liquid and poach, turning them frequently, until tender, 20–35 minutes; the timing will depend upon the ripeness of the pears.

✹ Using a slotted spoon, transfer the pears to a bowl. Reduce the cooking liquid over medium-high heat to ¾ cup (6 fl oz/180 ml), about 20 minutes. Remove from the heat.

✹ In a blender, combine the thawed raspberries and half of the reduced cooking liquid and process until smooth. Strain through a fine-mesh sieve placed over a bowl, pressing hard on the solids with the back of a spoon to extract as much juice as possible.

✹ To serve, place the pears in individual bowls. Spoon the remaining cooking liquid over the pears, dividing equally. Add a scoop (½ cup/ 4 fl oz/125 ml) of frozen yogurt to each bowl and drizzle 2 tablespoons of the raspberry sauce over each scoop. Reserve the remaining sauce for another use. Garnish with the fresh raspberries and the mint sprigs. Serve at once.

NUTRITIONAL ANALYSIS PER SERVING: Calories 307 (Kilojoules 1298); Protein 3 g; Carbohydrates 74 g; Total Fat 1 g; Saturated Fat 0 g; Cholesterol 0 mg; Sodium 51 mg; Dietary Fiber 5 g

Double Raspberry Soufflé

PREP TIME: 10 MINUTES

COOKING TIME: 15 MINUTES

INGREDIENTS

sugar for coating, plus 2½ tablespoons
    sugar

1½ cups (6 oz/185 g) fresh raspberries

1 package (10 oz/315 g) frozen
    raspberries in syrup, thawed

2 teaspoons lemon juice

4 egg whites

pinch of cream of tartar

1 tablespoon Cointreau or other
    orange liqueur

1 teaspoon vanilla extract (essence)

These individual soufflés take longer to bake than to assemble. As they come out of the oven, dust the tops with confectioners' (icing) sugar and serve with extra berries, if desired.

SERVES 6

❀ Preheat an oven to 375°F (190°C). Coat six ⅔-cup (5–fl oz/160-ml) soufflé molds with nonstick cooking spray. Then coat the molds with sugar, tapping out any excess. Divide the fresh berries among the soufflé molds; there should be 10–12 berries in each mold.

❀ Place the thawed raspberries in a blender and process just until smooth. Pass the berries through a fine-mesh sieve placed over a bowl, pressing hard on the solids with the back of a spoon to extract as much juice as possible. Transfer the purée to a small saucepan and add the 2½ tablespoons sugar and the lemon juice. Place over medium heat, bring to a simmer, and simmer for about 3 minutes.

❀ Meanwhile, in a bowl, using an electric mixer, beat together the egg whites and cream of tartar until stiff peaks form.

❀ Remove the purée from the heat and stir in the Cointreau and vanilla. Immediately pour the hot purée into the egg whites. Continue to beat just until the purée is incorporated.

❀ Spoon the purée mixture into the soufflé molds, dividing it evenly and filling them to the top. Smooth the tops, then run a thumb completely around the outer edge of the purée mixture to form a shallow indentation alongside the rim.

❀ Bake until puffed and golden brown on top, about 12 minutes. Remove from the oven and serve immediately.

NUTRITIONAL ANALYSIS PER SERVING: Calories 123 (Kilojoules 517); Protein 3 g; Carbohydrates 26 g; Total Fat 1 g; Saturated Fat 0 g; Cholesterol 0 mg; Sodium 37 mg; Dietary Fiber 1 g

Honey, Blood Orange, and Buttermilk Sorbet

PREP TIME: 10 MINUTES,
PLUS 3 HOURS FOR CHILL-
ING, CHURNING, AND
FREEZING

COOKING TIME: 2 MINUTES

INGREDIENTS

1 cup (8 fl oz/250 ml) blood orange
juice

⅓ cup (4 oz/125 g) honey

zest from 2 blood oranges

2 teaspoons unflavored gelatin

1½ cups (12 fl oz/375 ml) low-fat
buttermilk

2 teaspoons lemon juice

2 teaspoons vanilla extract (essence)

PREP TIP: A vegetable peeler is the
perfect tool for removing long strips
of zest (colored portion only) from
orange rinds.

If blood oranges are unavailable, you can substitute navel
oranges, but they lack the lovely fuchsia blush and sweet perfume
of blood oranges. Serve with fresh figs, if desired.

SERVES 6

❊ In a small saucepan over low heat, combine the orange juice, honey,
orange zest, and gelatin. Stir until the gelatin dissolves, about 2 minutes.

❊ Strain the hot mixture through a fine-mesh sieve placed over a bowl.
Stir in the buttermilk, lemon juice, and vanilla. Cover and chill for 1 hour.

❊ Transfer the orange juice mixture to an ice cream maker and process
according to the manufacturer's instructions. Transfer to a freezer container, cover tightly, and freeze until firm, about 2 hours.

❊ To serve, scoop or spoon into small glass serving dishes.

NUTRITIONAL ANALYSIS PER SERVING: Calories 117 (Kilojoules 491); Protein 3 g;
Carbohydrates 25 g; Total Fat 1 g; Saturated Fat 0 g; Cholesterol 4 mg; Sodium 91 mg;
Dietary Fiber 0 g

Mocha Cake with Caramel-Spiced Sauce

PREP TIME: 20 MINUTES

COOKING TIME: 40 MINUTES,
   PLUS 1 HOUR FOR COOLING

INGREDIENTS

1 cup (8 oz/250 g) sugar

½ cup (4 fl oz/125 ml) water

1 tablespoon instant espresso powder

3 oz (90 g) bittersweet chocolate, chopped

2 egg yolks

1 tablespoon brandy

1 tablespoon vanilla extract (essence)

⅔ cup (2 oz/60 g) unsweetened cocoa powder

⅓ cup (2 oz/60 g) all-purpose (plain) flour

5 egg whites

FOR THE SAUCE

½ cup (4 oz/125 g) sugar

3 tablespoons water

2 tablespoons fat-free sour cream

¼ teaspoon ground cinnamon

⅛ teaspoon ground mace

You will be surprised to discover that this fudgy cake contains no butter, oil, or shortening. The sauce provides all the "icing" needed.

SERVES 12

❀ Preheat an oven to 350°F (180°C). Coat a 9-inch (23-cm) springform cake pan with nonstick cooking spray.

❀ In a small saucepan over low heat, stir together the sugar, water, and espresso powder until the sugar dissolves, about 2 minutes. Whisk in the chocolate, egg yolks, brandy, and vanilla until the chocolate is melted and smooth, about 1 minute. Remove from the heat.

❀ In a large bowl, sift together the cocoa and flour. Stir in the chocolate mixture. In a bowl, using an electric mixer, beat the whites just until stiff peaks form. Fold them into the batter. Pour the batter into the prepared pan.

❀ Bake until the center of the surface looks dry and a toothpick inserted into the cake comes out with some sticky batter attached, about 35 minutes. Transfer the cake to a rack to let cool completely in the pan.

❀ Meanwhile, make the sauce: In a small saucepan over medium heat, stir together the sugar and 2 tablespoons of the water until the sugar dissolves, about 2 minutes. Cook, without stirring, until the mixture turns a dark amber, about 6 minutes. Using a pastry brush dipped in water, brush down the sides of the pan to remove any sugar crystals that form. Remove from the heat and stir in the sour cream, the remaining 1 tablespoon water, the cinnamon, and the mace. Whisk until the mixture is smooth. Let cool to room temperature.

❀ Release the pan sides and cut the cake into slices. Serve on individual plates. Drizzle some of the sauce over each slice.

NUTRITIONAL ANALYSIS PER SERVING: Calories 200 (Kilojoules 840); Protein 4 g; Carbohydrates 39 g; Total Fat 4 g; Saturated Fat 2 g; Cholesterol 36 mg; Sodium 28 mg; Dietary Fiber 2 g

Nectarine and Peach Gratin with Cinnamon Sabayon

PREP TIME: 20 MINUTES

COOKING TIME: 15 MINUTES

INGREDIENTS

3 large peaches, halved, pitted, and each cut into 12 wedges

3 large nectarines, halved, pitted, and each cut into 8 wedges

1 cup (4 oz/125 g) blueberries

¾ cup (6 fl oz/180 ml) sweet Muscat wine

3 tablespoons honey

3 eggs

1 tablespoon minced orange zest

¾ teaspoon ground cinnamon

COOKING TIP: Be sure to cook the egg mixture over simmering—not boiling—water. Otherwise, you will end up with custard instead of a light and frothy sabayon.

Any combination of ripe fruits, particularly the juicy varieties of summer, will marry well with this cinnamon and orange sabayon. A sweet Muscat wine delivers a wonderful flavor, but any sweet dessert wine could be substituted.

SERVES 6

❈ In a large bowl, toss together the peaches, nectarines, and blueberries. Divide the fruit evenly among six 1-cup (8–fl oz/250-ml) gratin dishes and place on a baking sheet. Preheat a broiler (griller).

❈ Pour water to a depth of 3 inches (7.5 cm) into a saucepan and bring to a gentle simmer over medium-low heat.

❈ Meanwhile, in a heatproof bowl, whisk together the wine, honey, eggs, orange zest, and cinnamon. Place the bowl over (not touching) the barely simmering water in the pan. Whisk constantly until the egg mixture triples in volume and is thick and foamy, about 8 minutes. Remove from the heat and spoon over the fruit to cover completely.

❈ Broil (grill) about 4 inches (10 cm) from the heat source until golden, about 3 minutes. Remove from the broiler and serve at once.

NUTRITIONAL ANALYSIS PER SERVING: Calories 205 (Kilojoules 861); Protein 5 g; Carbohydrates 34 g; Total Fat 3 g; Saturated Fat 1 g; Cholesterol 106 mg; Sodium 36 mg; Dietary Fiber 3 g

Pistachio and Almond Macaroons

PREP TIME: 20 MINUTES

COOKING TIME: 1½ HOURS

INGREDIENTS

¼ cup (1 oz/30 g) finely chopped
    pistachios

2 tablespoons ground, toasted
    almonds

1 tablespoon cornstarch (cornflour)

3 egg whites

¼ teaspoon rose water

¼ cup (2 oz/60 g) sugar

COOKING TIP: If the cookies become
soft during storage, return them to
a preheated 200°F (95°C) oven for
10 minutes, then let cool until crisp.

The flavor of pistachios and rose water makes these little cookies
a good ending to an Indian meal. Look for rose water, an essence
distilled from fresh rose petals, in specialty-food stores. Serve
the macaroons with fat-free vanilla frozen yogurt.

MAKES 25 COOKIES

❀ Position a rack in the upper third of an oven and preheat to 325°F
(165°C). Coat a large baking sheet with nonstick cooking spray.

❀ In a small bowl, stir together the pistachios, almonds, and cornstarch.
Fit a pastry bag with a ½-inch (12-mm) star tip. In a large bowl, using
an electric mixer, beat together the egg whites and rose water until soft
peaks form. Gradually beat in the sugar until stiff peaks form. Using a
rubber spatula, gently fold the nut mixture into the whites just until
evenly distributed.

❀ Spoon the egg whites into the pastry bag, then pipe kisses 2 inches
(5 cm) wide on the prepared baking sheet, spacing them evenly.

❀ Bake until golden brown and set, about 25 minutes. Turn off the oven
and let the cookies stand in the oven with the door closed for 1 hour.

❀ Using a metal spatula, gently remove the cookies to a rack to cool.
Serve the cookies, or store in an airtight container at room temperature
for up to 5 days.

NUTRITIONAL ANALYSIS PER COOKIE: Calories 22 (Kilojoules 92); Protein 1 g;
Carbohydrates 3 g; Total Fat 1 g; Saturated Fat 0 g; Cholesterol 0 mg; Sodium 7 mg; Dietary
Fiber 0 g

Mango, Lime, and Coconut Mousse

PREP TIME: 20 MINUTES,
PLUS 6 HOURS FOR
CHILLING

COOKING TIME: 1 MINUTE

INGREDIENTS

1½ lb (750 g) mangoes

1½ teaspoons unflavored gelatin

3½ tablespoons fresh lime juice

2 tablespoons sugar

¼ teaspoon coconut extract (essence)

½ cup (4 fl oz/125 ml) fat-free
   evaporated skimmed milk, chilled

2 tablespoons flaked coconut

fresh mint sprigs for garnish

PREP TIP: A whisk is a better tool
than an electric mixer for whipping
the evaporated milk.

This mousse delivers a cool tropical taste. It can be made up to
3 days in advance; keep in the refrigerator until serving. For a tip
on preparing mangoes, see page 70.

SERVES 4

❀ Place a bowl in the freezer to chill. Peel the mangoes and cut the flesh
from the pits.

❀ In a small saucepan, sprinkle the gelatin over the lime juice and let
stand for 5 minutes. Place over low heat and stir until the gelatin dissolves, about 1 minute. Remove from the heat.

❀ In a food processor or blender, combine the mangoes, gelatin mixture,
sugar, and coconut extract and process until smooth. Pour the mango
purée into a large bowl.

❀ Remove the chilled bowl from the freezer and pour the evaporated
milk into it. Using a whisk, beat until thick and foamy, about 5 minutes.
Fold the evaporated milk into the mango purée just until no white
streaks remain.

❀ Divide the mousse among four ¾-cup (6–fl oz/180-ml) bowls. Cover
and refrigerate until set, about 6 hours.

❀ While the mousse is chilling, preheat an oven to 350°F (180°C). Spread
the coconut in a small pan and toast in the oven until golden, about
3 minutes. Remove from the oven and let cool.

❀ Just before serving, remove the molds from the refrigerator and sprinkle
one-fourth of the coconut over each one. Garnish with mint and serve.

NUTRITIONAL ANALYSIS PER SERVING: Calories 143 (Kilojoules 601); Protein 4 g;
Carbohydrates 32 g; Total Fat 1 g; Saturated Fat 1 g; Cholesterol 1 mg; Sodium 49 mg;
Dietary Fiber 1 g

Chocolate Meringue "Pies"

PREP TIME: 30 MINUTES, PLUS
1 HOUR FOR FREEZING

COOKING TIME: 2 HOURS

INGREDIENTS

2 egg whites

½ cup (4 oz/125 g) sugar

2 tablespoons unsweetened cocoa
powder

1 pint (16 fl oz/500 ml) fat-free
chocolate sorbet, softened

¼ cup (1¼ oz/37 g) chopped bittersweet chocolate

1½ tablespoons chopped fresh mint

These treats, based on the old-fashioned "Moon Pies," have been nicknamed the World's Greatest After-Dinner Mint. Chocolate sorbet is sandwiched between chocolate meringue disks and rolled in a mix of bittersweet chocolate and fresh mint.

SERVES 6

❀ Preheat an oven to 250°F (120°C). Line a baking sheet with parchment (baking) paper. Trace twelve 3-inch (7.5-cm) circles on the parchment paper.

❀ In a bowl, using an electric mixer, beat the egg whites until soft peaks form. Gradually add the sugar and continue beating until stiff peaks form. Using a rubber spatula, fold the cocoa into the whites until combined.

❀ Fit a pastry bag with a ¼-inch (6-mm) plain tip. Spoon the egg whites into the bag. Pipe concentric circles into each traced 3-inch (7.5-cm) circle to fill completely.

❀ Bake the meringues until dry, about 2 hours. Remove from the oven and, using a narrow-bladed metal spatula, gently pry the meringues from the parchment paper.

❀ Place ⅓ cup (3 fl oz/80 ml) of the sorbet on the bottom of 1 disk. Gently press the sorbet with the spatula to spread it to the edges of the disk. Top with a second disk, bottom down, and smooth the edges with the spatula. Place on a baking sheet and place in the freezer. Repeat with the remaining disks and sorbet, add them to the baking sheet, and freeze until firm, about 1 hour.

❀ Just before serving, on a sheet of waxed paper, mix together the chocolate and chopped mint. Roll the edges of each "pie" in the choco- late mixture. Serve immediately.

NUTRITIONAL ANALYSIS PER SERVING: Calories 205 (Kilojoules 861); Protein 3 g; Carbohydrates 44 g; Total Fat 3 g; Saturated Fat 1 g; Cholesterol 0 mg; Sodium 73 mg; Dietary Fiber 2 g

Caramelized Spiced Apple Tartlets

PREP TIME: 30 MINUTES

COOKING TIME: 45 MINUTES,
  PLUS 20 MINUTES FOR
  COOLING

INGREDIENTS

2 sheets filo dough, thawed
  in the refrigerator if frozen

1 cup (8 fl oz/250 ml) apple juice

3 tablespoons plus 2 teaspoons
  golden brown sugar

4 apples, peeled, cored, and cut into
  slices ½ inch (12 mm) thick

1 teaspoon pumpkin pie spice

2 tablespoons dried currants

Serve these individual tarts with a dollop of fromage blanc that
has been spiked with sugar, vanilla extract (essence), and
chopped fresh mint. Garnish with mint sprigs, if desired.

SERVES 4

❀ Preheat an oven to 350°F (180°C).

❀ Cut the filo sheets in half crosswise. Stack the half sheets one on
top of the other. Using a 4-inch (10-cm) circular cookie cutter, cut out
4 rounds from the stack. Cover all but 1 stack of rounds with a kitchen
towel. Dissemble the stack and brush apple juice on 1 round. Sprinkle
with ¼ teaspoon brown sugar. Top with a second round, brush with apple
juice, and again sprinkle with ¼ teaspoon sugar. Top with the third round.
Repeat with the juice and sugar on the fourth round. Coat a baking pan
with nonstick cooking spray. Place the filo stack on the prepared baking
sheet, and coat the stack with nonstick cooking spray. Repeat the proce-
dure with the remaining filo stacks, spacing them evenly apart on the
baking sheet. Place a second baking sheet on top of the assembled stacks
to keep them flat while they bake.

❀ Place the sandwiched filo stacks in the oven and bake until crisp and
golden, about 8 minutes. Remove from the oven and transfer the stacks
to a rack to cool.

❀ Meanwhile, heat a large nonstick frying pan over medium heat. Coat
with nonstick cooking spray. Add the apples, 2 tablespoons of the sugar,
and the pumpkin pie spice and sauté until golden, about 10 minutes.
Add the remaining ¾ cup (6 fl oz/180 ml) apple juice and the currants.
Cook until the apples caramelize and the liquid evaporates, about 20 minutes. Remove from the heat and let cool completely, about 20 minutes.
Preheat a broiler (griller).

❀ Arrange the apple mixture decoratively atop the filo stacks, dividing
it evenly. Sprinkle ¼ teaspoon sugar over each tartlet. Place the tartlets on
a baking sheet and slip under the broiler about 4 inches (10 cm) from
the heat source. Broil (grill) until the sugar bubbles, about 2 minutes.
Remove from the broiler and serve immediately.

NUTRITIONAL ANALYSIS PER SERVING: Calories 177 (Kilojoules 743); Protein 1 g;
Carbohydrates 41 g; Total Fat 2 g; Saturated Fat 0 g; Cholesterol 0 mg; Sodium 40 mg;
Dietary Fiber 3 g

GLOSSARY

ARROWROOT

Flavorless and easy to digest, arrowroot is an excellent fat-free thickener for soups, sauces, and puddings. To disperse arrowroot uniformly through a sauce, dissolve it first in a small quantity of cold liquid. Because its thickening power diminishes with age, buy arrowroot in small quantities and store it in an airtight container.

ARUGULA

This spicy, slightly bitter green, also known as rocket, is native to the Mediterranean, where it is standard salad-bowl fare. The long, multi-lobed leaves hide grit and must be washed well before using. Dunk the leaves in a bowl of cold water, let them stand a moment, and then gently lift out; the sand will fall to the bottom of the bowl.

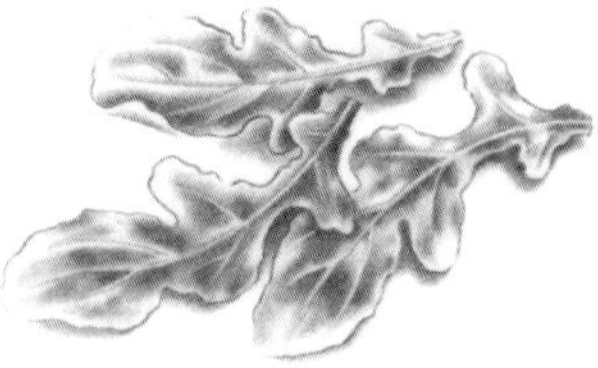

ASPARAGUS

Tender shoots of asparagus start pushing up through the earth in early spring and reach their peak of flavor in May. Choose asparagus with tightly closed buds and with stem ends that look freshly cut.

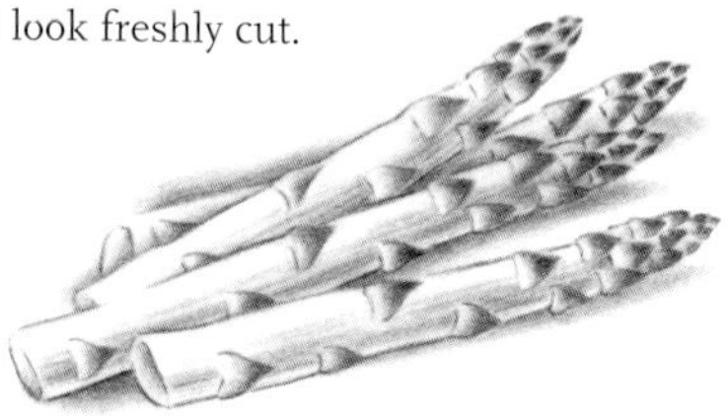

BELL PEPPERS, RED

As they ripen, bell peppers, also known as capsicums, change from green to red, and their flavor changes from sharp to sweet. Look for peppers that are firm, heavy for their size, smooth, and glossy.

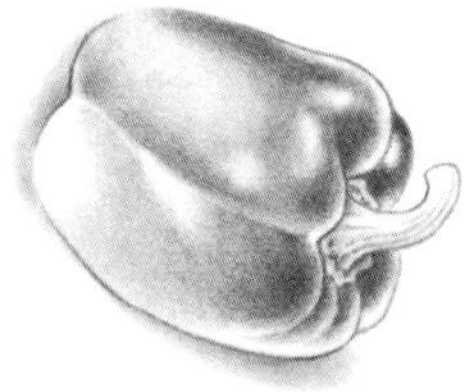

BUTTERMILK

True buttermilk is the liquid that remains in the churn after butter has been made. Commercial buttermilk is made by introducing a bacterial culture to nonfat or low-fat milk. Buttermilk lends richness and flavor to foods with a minimum of fat.

EVAPORATED SKIM MILK

A vacuum is employed to evaporate rapidly almost half of the water from milk, resulting in a product with a more intense flavor, thicker consistency, and longer shelf life than regular milk. This richer-tasting milk can be used to enhance sauces, baked goods, and desserts, and can also be whipped. The increasing demand for low-fat foods has led manufacturers of evaporated milk to offer reduced-fat and fat-free versions.

EXTRACTS

Vanilla beans, almonds, and peppermint leaves are some of the common ingredients used to make extracts (essences). For the richest, truest flavor, look for extracts labeled "pure" or "natural," except when buying coconut extract, which is produced only in imitation form.

FENNEL

Looking remarkably like a small head of celery squashed down into a fat bulb, fennel is paler green than celery but has the same

CHILES

Scores of chile varieties exist in a wide range of shapes, sizes, and colors. Some are sweet, others are astringent, some are surprisingly mild. Weather and growing conditions affect heat levels, and it's not unusual for a presumably mild chile to turn out hot or vice versa. In the case of all chiles, the heat is concentrated in the interior ribs and in the seeds because of their proximity to the ribs. Scraping off the ribs and discarding the seeds can make a hot chile less so. You'll find the best selection of chiles at Latin American, Asian, and farmers' markets. Those used in this book include:

ANAHEIM

This slender, rather flat green chile may be mild or slightly hot. It is sometimes referred to as long green or California chile.

ANCHO

In Spanish, *ancho* means "wide," a reference to this dried chile's broad shape. Known as the poblano in its fresh form, the ancho has brick-red, wrinkled skin and a spicy, but not necessarily hot, sweet, fruity flavor.

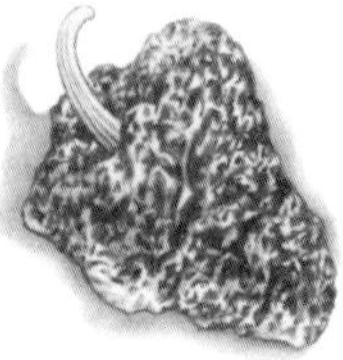

CHIPOTLE

The jalapeño, which does not take well to air drying, is instead dried by means of smoke, at which point it is called a chipotle. Rich and aromatic, with the flavor of sweet smoke, this fiery chile is hot but not at all astringent. Chipotles are sold loose, canned in vinegar, or, most commonly, canned in a thick vinegar-based sauce called adobo.

JALAPEÑO

This familiar fresh green, or less often red, chile ranges from medium-hot to very hot and has thick, juicy, slightly sweet flesh.

stringy outer layer. The texture is clean and crisp, and the flavor is reminiscent of mild, sweet anise. Look for bulbs with the feathery leaves intact. The leaves can give a fresh spark to green salads or be used as a seasoning or garnish.

FROMAGE BLANC
Literally "white cheese," this French term refers to a wide variety of unripened creamy cheeses. Commercial products vary in fat content, although many low-fat varieties are available. To make your own nonfat version, stir together 1 cup (8 oz/250 g) each nonfat plain yogurt and fat-free cottage cheese. Transfer to a sieve set over a bowl and allow to drain at room temperature for about 3½ hours. Discard the captured liquid. Process the cheese in a blender or food processor until smooth, then press through a fine sieve into a storage container, cover, and refrigerate; use within 7–10 days.

GINGER
Although it resembles a root, this sweet-hot seasoning is actually the underground stem, or rhizome, of the tropical ginger plant. Some recipes call for thinly sliced or shredded ginger pickled in vinegar, which is available in Japanese or Chinese markets.

LEEKS
Succulent, sweet, and with a delicate onion flavor, leeks arrive in the market in late summer and extend their stay through spring. The blanched white base, more tender and more delicately flavored than the green leaves, is most often used alone. The tougher green

HERBS
Intensely aromatic and packed with flavor, herbs bring a rich, graceful note to whatever they season.

CHIVES
When you are seeking an onionlike flavor without the bite, reach for chives. Mild and sweet, chives are at their best when raw, as cooking diminishes their flavor.

CILANTRO
Also known as fresh coriander and Chinese parsley, cilantro has flat, frilly leaves that resemble those of flat-leaf (Italian) parsley. Its flavor is pungent, slightly grassy, and a little bitter.

DILL
Anyone who has ever eaten a dill pickle knows the sprightly taste of this feathery-leaved herb. Its delicate aroma is lost when the leaves are dried or cooked, so buy the freshest dill you can find (the leaves and stems should be bright green) and add it to dishes just before serving.

HERBES DE PROVENCE
This blend of dried herbs is a typical seasoning of Provence in south-central France. The mix varies with the home cook or commercial packager. If you wish to make your own, here is a common blend: combine 3 parts each crumbled dried thyme and basil;

2 parts each crumbled dried marjoram, rosemary, and lavender or chamomile blossoms, and 1 part each ground dried sage and crushed fennel seeds. Transfer to a glass jar, cover tightly, and store in a cool, dark place.

PARSLEY, FLAT-LEAF
Also known as Italian parsley, this variety of the widely popular fresh herb, native to southern Europe, has a more pronounced flavor than the common curly type, making it preferable as a seasoning.

SAGE
Soft, gray-green sage leaves are pungent and aromatic. They go especially well with poultry, vegetables, and pork.

TARRAGON
The peppery, aniselike taste of tarragon enhances salads and a wide variety of mild foods such as chicken and fish.

THYME
One of the most important culinary herbs of Europe, thyme delivers a light fragrance and subtle flavor to all types of food. It goes particularly well with mild cheeses, vegetables, and nearly every meat or fish.

portion can be used to flavor stocks or included in long-cooked dishes. Leeks grow in sandy soil. Once chopped, they should be rinsed thoroughly in cold water to remove any grit trapped in their multilayered leaves.

MANGO

Sweet, dense, and full of juice, the flesh of a fully ripe mango is as tender as a ripe avocado. To test for ripeness, sniff the stem end; you should smell a

pleasant perfume. If the smell is at all sour, the fruit has passed its prime and begun to ferment.

NONSTICK COOKING SPRAY

Spraying cooking surfaces with this mixture of cooking oil, lecithin (a soy-derived emulsifying agent), a harmless propellant, and occasionally grain alcohol allows cooks to sauté and grill without the addition of a significant amount of fat. Use caution when spraying near a heated stovetop or open flame. The can may burst if left on the stove or near a heat source.

OILS

A variety of good-quality oils play a fundamental role in the kitchens of even the most fat-conscious cooks.

CORN OIL

Nearly tasteless, corn oil can be heated to a high temperature without burning, making it an excellent all-purpose cooking oil.

HAZELNUT OIL

Just a few drops of this intensely flavored oil gives a rich, nutty taste to food. Nut oils can go rancid quickly, so buy them in small quantities and store in the refrigerator.

MUSHROOMS

With their earthy flavor and satisfyingly chewy texture, mushrooms of all sorts can lend a robust, meaty quality to low-fat meals. You'll find familiar cultivated varieties at well-stocked food stores, greengrocers, and farmers' markets alongside many wild varieties—some of which are now commercially grown.

When preparing mushrooms, avoid washing them (with the exception of morels); instead, use a mushroom brush or damp kitchen towel to wipe off any dirt.

CHANTERELLE

This golden, trumpet-shaped mushroom can range in flavor from mild and meaty to softly spicy, nutty, and floral. The season for chanterelles begins in summer and lasts through winter.

CREMINI

An earthy brown cap, firmer texture, and richer flavor distinguish these cultivated mushrooms from their more commonplace white kin.

ENOKI

Fruity and slightly acidic, Japanese enoki have long, skinny stems and tiny caps. Their crisp texture and subtle aroma are best enjoyed raw.

MOREL

Hollow-stemmed with oval honeycombed caps, morels look like trees in a fairy-tale forest. These much-loved wild mushrooms make their appearance in spring when they are gathered in the woodlands of New England, Michigan, and the Pacific Northwest. The meshlike flesh and empty core of the cap provide a hiding place for dirt and debris from the forest floor. Rinse well before

cooking, or even soak briefly if necessary, then trim the stems before using.

OYSTER

Delicate flesh as soft as chamois puts the oyster mushroom in a class by itself. Its flavor is extremely subtle and the texture is almost meltingly tender. Oyster mushrooms are quite perishable, so try to use them soon after purchase.

SHIITAKE

Parasol-like shiitake mushrooms were once found only in Asia but are now cultivated all over the world. The broad, flat caps have a firm, meaty texture. Discard the tough stems before using.

OLIVE OIL

No one adjective describes the range of tastes possible in olive oils. Some are spicy with a peppery kick, others buttery and mellow. Those labeled "extra virgin" are generally fruity and full flavored and are suitable for dressing salads and for using as a condiment. Oils labeled "pure" are blended and more refined and are useful for cooking.

SESAME OIL

The nutty fragrance of Asian sesame oil, made from roasted sesame seeds, enhances not only Asian food, but many Western dishes as well. Used primarily as a seasoning or condiment, Asian sesame oil burns easily and is rarely used for cooking. The Asian product should not be confused with the lighter, cold-pressed sesame oil sold in health-food stores and well-stocked food stores.

SHALLOTS

These coppery-skinned cousins of the onion have a more delicate flavor than their sharper kin. The finely textured flesh is commonly used as an aromatic seasoning.

SOUR CREAM

Traditionally made from sweet cream inoculated with a bacterial culture, sour cream is now available in nonfat versions. Read labels carefully and be sure to choose true dairy products rather than imitation sour cream.

SOY SAUCE

Fermented soybeans, wheat, salt, and water are the basis for this staple seasoning of Asian cuisine. The best soy sauce has a rich aroma and a taste that is both salty and pungent. Those labeled "light" are lighter in color and flavor. To reduce the amount of salt in your diet, seek out low-sodium soy sauce.

SPICES

Aromatic seeds, berries, buds, roots, and bark are all used as spices. For the best flavor, buy whole spices whenever possible and grind them as needed in an electric spice mill or in a mortar with a pestle. Some used in this book include:

CUMIN

Cooks in Mexico, India, the Middle East, and the American Southwest regularly use cumin to flavor dishes. These potent seeds have a strong, slightly smoky flavor that's difficult to define but unmistakable once you know it.

CURRY POWDER

A blend of spices most often used to season Indian dishes. Common components include coriander, cumin, chile, fenugreek, and turmeric. Sometimes cardamom, cinnamon, cloves, allspice, fennel seeds, and ginger are also added.

FIVE-SPICE POWDER

This intriguing mixture, usually made up of star anise, fennel or aniseeds, cloves, cinnamon, and Sichuan peppercorns, is primarily used in Chinese and Vietnamese kitchens.

SAFFRON

In order to reap just 1 pound (500 g) of saffron, laborers must pluck the three hairlike stigma from over 75,000 crocus blossoms. This arduous harvest is the reason that saffron is one of the world's most expensive spices. Fortunately, the dried stigmas, known as threads, are so flavorful that adding just a few delivers a wealth of flavor. Saffron loses flavor quickly once it has been crushed, so buy only whole threads.

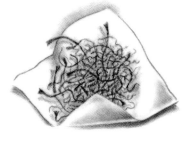

TURMERIC

This popular Asian spice has a mildly pungent, earthy flavor and lends its bright yellow color to whatever it seasons.

VINEGARS

Scientists claim that vinegar stimulates the taste buds, making them more responsive to a variety of flavors, and also aids digestion. Although wine is the basis of what are perhaps the most common vinegars, grains such as rice and barley, sugar cane, fruits, and even the sap of palm trees are also used.

BALSAMIC VINEGAR

Cooked grape juice, known as *musto cotto*, rather than wine is used to make this treasured Italian vinegar. The best balsamic vinegars have a finely balanced sweet-sour flavor.

RICE VINEGAR

The sediment that remains from the production of rice wine is the basis for this mild, slightly sweet vinegar, a Japanese staple. Bottles labeled "seasoned rice vinegar" contain products that have been flavored with salt and sugar.

SHERRY VINEGAR

A deep caramel color and rich, full flavor are characteristics of a fine sherry vinegar. Made from the fortified Spanish wine from which it takes its name, sherry vinegar is aged in a network of wooden casks known as *solera*.

WHITE WINE VINEGAR

Relatively mild when compared to other wine vinegars, white wine vinegar is the ideal choice when food needs only a light acidic touch.

YOGURT

Noted for its mildly acidic flavor and custard-like texture, yogurt is made from lightly fermented milk. In response to consumer demand for reduced-fat products, low-fat and nonfat yogurts are now widely available.

INDEX

ACKNOWLEDGMENTS

The publishers would like to thank the following people and associations for their assistance and support in producing this book: Ken DellaPenta, Jennifer Hanson, Hill Nutrition Associates, Sharilyn Hovind, Lisa Lee, and Cecily Upton.

The following kindly lent props for photography: Fillamento, Williams-Sonoma, and Pottery Barn, San Francisco, CA. The photographer would like to thank Jon and Caryn Schulberg for generously sharing their home with us for our location setting. We would also like to thank Chromeworks and ProCamera, San Francisco, CA, and FUJI Film for their generous support of this project. Special acknowledgment goes to Daniel Yearwood for the beautiful backgrounds and surface treatments.